CENTER FOR INTERNATIONAL STUDIES
MASSACHUSETTS INSTITUTE OF TECHNOLOGY

STUDIES IN ELECTORAL POLITICS
IN THE INDIAN STATES

Edited by Myron Weiner & John Osgood Field

VOL. I

ELECTORAL POLITICS IN THE INDIAN STATES

The Communist Parties of West Bengal

STUDIES IN ELECTORAL POLITICS IN THE INDIAN STATES

Edited by Myron Weiner & John Osgood Field

OTHER VOLUMES IN THE SERIES

Studies in Electoral Politics in the Indian States Vol. I

ELECTORAL POLITICS IN THE INDIAN STATES

The Communist Parties of West Bengal

JOHN OSGOOD FIELD
and
MARCUS F. FRANDA

MANOHAR BOOK SERVICE

1974

First Published 1974
© Massachusetts Institute of Technology

Distributors for U. S. A.
South Asia Books
Box 502
Columbia, Mo 65201

Published by
Ramesh C. Jain for
Manohar Book Service
2, Daryaganj, Ansari Road
Panna Bhawan
Delhi-110006

Printed by
Prem Printing Press
257-Golaganj
Lucknow-226001

INTRODUCTION

The M. I. T. Indian Election Data Project was begun in early 1968 initially under a pilot grant from the Center for International Studies, followed by a major grant from the National Science Foundation, with the objective of undertaking a series of computer-based studies of elections in India since 1952 in the more than 3,000 state assembly constituencies. The early ambitious hope was that these studies could bring to the analysis of Indian elections some of the methodologies and sophisticated statistical tools that have been developed for the study of elections in the United States and other developed countries, test with the Indian electoral data some of the general propositions that have emerged in recent studies of political development, improve our knowledge of the world's largest democratic state, and enhance our capacity to predict future electoral change in India.

The technical dimensions of this project proved to be so formidable that at times we despaired of producing any studies! The data had to be computerized, "cleaned," and checked for inconsistencies. They then had to be arranged in files, concepts had to be converted into measures, and innumerable problems of how to compare constituencies with one another and with themselves over time had to be resolved. At an early stage in the project we considered matching selected census data to constituencies in order to relate some electoral variables such as turnout, competitiveness, and party performance to socio-economic variables but decided not to do so since a number of such studies were under way elsewhere—particularly the work of W. H. Morris-Jones and Biplab Das Gupta at the Institute for Commonwealth Studies in London, Rajni Kothari at the Centre for the Study of Developing Societies in Delhi, Paul Brass at the University of Washington, Harry Blair at Bucknell, and Donald Zagoria at Columbia University.

As the months, then years, passed and the technical problems grew, our research objectives became more limited. We settled on two modest goals: (1) to put the data in usable form and make it widely available to scholars in the United States and India; and (2) to conduct a number of pilot studies on themes that might prove of interest both to India area experts and to those with a broader concern with electoral behavior in developing countries, in order to illustrate some of the potential uses of the data.

Computer tapes containing the election data have been placed on file with the Indian Council for Social Science Research in New Delhi, at the Inter-University Consortium at the University of Michigan and at the

International Data Library at the University of California, Berkeley. These tapes contain the state election results by constituencies for each general election from 1952 through 1967, the mid-term elections of 1968-1969, and several earlier mid-term elections. (Some of the studies used 1971 and 1972 state election data, but since these are "unofficial" returns not yet published by the Indian Election Commission, we have not incorporated them into the permanent archives.) With the tapes is documentation explaining what the archives contain, how they are arranged, and how they can be used. They are available to scholars everywhere under the procedures established by each of these three centers.

Pilot studies were undertaken by members of the M. I. T. faculty and staff and by scholars at other universities. They fall into two principal groups. The first focuses on the relationship between electoral behavior and some aspects of modernization, taking as their starting point "all-India" problems or phenomena. These studies look at the electoral correlates of India's Green Revolution (Frankel), of varying rates and patterns of migration (Katzenstein), and of urbanization (Weiner and Field). A related group of studies examines changing voting patterns in two types of "backward" regions in India, areas that were formerly part of princely India (Richter) and areas in which tribals live (Weiner and Field). Another study examines the electoral performance of women candidates in state assembly elections (Desai and Bhagwati).

Most of these studies make some use of census and other socio-economic data; the urban study, for example, relates electoral characteristics to city size, the migration study to different patterns of migration, the Green Revolution study to agrarian conditions and their change, and the princely study to selected indices of development. But in the main these studies tend to treat the environment as space; they look not at how tribals voted, but at how tribal constituencies voted; not at how urban dwellers voted, but at how urban constituencies voted; and so on.

A major theme of several of these studies is the way in which national electoral trends intersect with regional variations, and the way in which specific categories of local constituencies are influenced by the state in which they are located. Thus, "princely," urban, and tribal constituencies each have characteristics of their own; but their electoral patterns are also strongly influenced on the one hand by the particular state in which they are located and by national trends on the other. One striking conclusion is that it is meaningless to characterize the electoral patterns of urban India as a whole, or migrant areas as a whole, or tribal India as a whole. In a country as diverse as India, all statistical differences are "washed out" in national averages. For the purpose of testing most theories of political participation, such as the relationship between social mobilization and political participation, the state and other component units are far more useful levels of analysis than is India at large, an important lesson for scholars doing cross-national aggregate analyses.

The second group of studies examines the major cleavages in Indian politics and their party and electoral manifestations. Divisions based on class, caste, tribe, religion, urban-rural differences, language, region, and factional alignments are the raw material of Indian political life. The pilot studies examine three types of cleavage politics in the party and electoral systems: ideological cleavages, focusing on the Communist parties of West Bengal (Field and Franda) and Kerala (Hardgrave); regional and ethnic cleavages, focusing on cultural nationalism in Tamil Nadu (Barnett) and religion-based parties in the Punjab (Brass); and caste-cum-factional rivalries in Uttar Pradesh (Baxter) and Mysore (Wood and Hammond). A major theme of these studies is the question of how institutionalized are individual parties and state party systems, that is, how dependable and persistent is the support for individual parties over several elections, and to what extent do voters give their support to "major" parties as opposed to frittering away their votes for smaller parties and independent candidates.

It is not possible to summarize here the many findings of these studies, but several can be mentioned: the importance of what can be called "proximity" variables, such as ethnic concentrations, railroad and river lines, and settlement clusters; the durable bases of party support in states like West Bengal, Kerala, and Tamil Nadu, but not in Uttar Pradesh, where "flash" parties are indicative of fragile voter loyalties; the mobilizing capacity of princely candidates and ethnic parties like the DMK in Tamil Nadu or the tribal Jharkhand Party in Bihar to increase voter turnout, but the inability of ideological parties with a class appeal to do the same; the surprisingly large margin of victory for most party candidates and the correspondingly few constituencies that are intensely competitive in terms of how the vote is distributed; and finally, the considerable amount of continuity in party support and electoral outcomes from one election to another, a possible measure of the extent to which Indian parties are institutionalized.

A major effort was made to develop and consistently use measures for the various concepts that were employed. These include measures of participation, competitiveness and bloc cohesion, party institutionalization, and party performance. Procedures were also devised for measuring the way in which votes are translated into seats, the success with which votes are "transferred" from one party to another over time, and how party swings take place, especially with regard to the gains and losses for incumbents.

Preliminary versions of most of these studies were presented in June 1972 at a seminar on electoral patterns in the Indian states held at the estate of the American Academy of Arts and Sciences in Brookline,

Massachusetts. We want to take this opportunity to express our appreciation to Baldev Raj Nayar of McGill University and to Walter Dean Burnham, Hayward Alker, and Douglas Hibbs of M. I. T. for participating in the seminar and providing helpful critical comments on the papers.

At M. I. T. this project has largely been a three-person enterprise which included, along with the director and co-director, our associate Priscilla Battis, who "interacted" with the computer and provided the printout for almost all of the studies in this series. Without her technical skills, organizing talents, and boundless energy we would not have achieved even our limited objectives. We should also like to express appreciation to James Wixson for his technical assistance and to Jessie Janjigian for editorial assistance as we approached publication. We are grateful to the National Science Foundation for making these investigations possible.

This study of the electoral performance of the Communist parties of West Bengal is the first publication in our series. The study focuses on the period from 1967, when the Communists in West Bengal joined a coalition government for the first time in the history of the state, to 1972 when Mrs. Gandhi's Congress Party reasserted its dominant position in the state. Though the Communists had previously taken power in the small southern state of Kerala, their electoral success in West Bengal, a populated, industrialized state bordering on Nepal and what was then Pakistan, and within not very many miles of the Chinese border, made them a new force in Indian politics. To some, Lenin's oft-quoted statement that the road to national power in India lay through Calcutta seemed remarkably prescient. Indeed, the growth of the Communist parties in these two states at a time when Prime Minister Indira Gandhi's Congress controlled only a plurality of seats in the national parliament, led many Indians to openly consider the possibility of a Congress-Communist coalition at the national level in the 1970's.

By 1972 the situation had changed. India had beaten Pakistan in a war over Bangladesh, a triumph likely to turn many Bengali voters to support the national government; supporters of Mrs. Gandhi were building a new organizational structure in West Bengal with a considerable following from many Bengali youths; internecine warfare among the three major Communist groups in West Bengal—the Communist Party of India, the Communist Party (Marxist), and the Communist Party (Marxist-Leninist) —had disillusioned many left-leaning Bengalis; and finally, during a period of President's Rule, and on the eve of the 1972 elections, the Indian army and police actively combated both the CPM and the CPML.

Nonetheless, some observers point to the success of the Communists in 1967, 1969, and 1971 as indicative of a leftist trend only temporarily halted by the events of the following year. For this reason it is particularly important to ask whether the growth of the Communist movement reflected shifting voter sentiments or was instead the consequence of electoral arrangements. Had the Communists finally broken out of the Calcutta industrial region into the West Bengal countryside and, if so, was this an indication of growing rural discontent? And why had the Communists grown at a time when they were bitterly split into pro-Soviet and pro-Chinese parties, each putting up its own candidates for the state legislative assembly?

These questions are posed and answered by Professors Field and Franda in their careful statistical analysis of electoral data for all state assembly constituencies in West Bengal during the elections of 1967, 1969, 1971, and 1972. Their results will surprise many readers. I shall avoid summarizing their remarkable findings here except to note that in these four elections the combined vote of the Communists has remained fairly constant and that, contrary to the belief of many in India and elsewhere, the two parties continue to remain confined largely to the industrial areas of the state. Field and Franda suggest why this is so and then show how the two Communist parties have been able to parlay their own split into occasionally effective coalition politics in the state.

This well-reasoned, precise analysis not only demonstrates what can be learned about *party* behaviour through a careful statistical analysis of computerized electoral data, but it also shows the merits of combining field experience with computer expertise. Professor Franda has worked in West Bengal for over a decade, first unraveling the complex pattern of state-centre relations and more recently looking at the even more complex elements of leftist party politics in the state. He is the author of *Radical Politics in West Bengal* (Cambridge, Mass. : MIT Press, 1972). Dr Field, who is co-director of the Indian Election Data Project at M. I. T., is himself no stranger to India. Earlier this year he completed a detailed analysis of politicization and the development of party affiliations in Indian society. Both scholars have sought to avoid the display of technical virtuosity so often associated with computer studies; they are concerned with making machine-readable data human-readable as well.

October 1973   *Myron Weiner*

ACKNOWLEDGEMENTS

This study originated as a pilot exploration of the data on Indian elections collected by Myron Weiner and his associates at the Center for International Studies and filed for computer processing at the Massachusetts Institute of Technology. The authors thought it best to begin analysis of the data with a limited focus: an electoral profile of one or two parties in one Indian state which might later be expanded to a profile of different political parties at the national level. The immediate purpose of this undertaking was to test the feasibility of analyzing the electoral performance of various parties in India in accordance with our preliminary notions of what could and should be examined with the data at hand, while bringing into the open some of the inevitable methodological problems that arise when working with such data.

What appears in this volume is at least a partial fulfillment of our initial goals, and there are many people and institutions to whom we owe a sincere debt of gratitude for assisting us along the way. We wish to thank Professors Myron Weiner and William E. Griffith for their roles in making this study possible. We should also like to record our appreciation to Priscilla Battis and James Wixson for the elaborate data preparation on which the analysis rests, and to Vonnie Franda for drawing the maps, proofreading, and for otherwise making cheerful a most time-consuming project. The constructive criticism of Dr. Rajni Kothari and his colleagues at the Centre for the Study of Developing Societies in Delhi has been of great help to us, as has that of Professor Walter Dean Burnham at M.I.T. We are grateful to the American Universities Field Staff for permission to quote from the Field Staff Report by Franda entitled "Calcutta and the New Congress Government," 1972 (Vol. 17, No. 1). An earlier version of this study was presented by Field at the Annual Meeting of the Association of Asian Studies held at the Waldorf-Astoria Hotel, New York City, in March 1972.

Our names appear on the title page in alphabetical order, perhaps the only way to summarize a lengthy association and genuinely collaborative research to which each contributed vitally.

CONTENTS

LIST OF TABLES

LIST OF FIGURES

ELECTORAL POLITICS IN THE INDIAN STATES : THE COMMUNIST PARTIES OF WEST BENGAL

I. Introduction

Politics in West Bengal is not normally associated with an electoral process. Although elections have been held more frequently in West Bengal than in any other Indian state, interest in Bengali politics has tended to focus on such dramatic events as the terrorism of the nationalist movement, the wave of communal killings that accompanied the partition of India in 1947, the insurrection launched by the Communist Party of India after Indian independence, the sporadic flare-ups of violence in Calcutta in the 1950's and early 1960's, and more recently the Naxalite uprisings of the late 1960's and the Bangladesh agitation of the early 1970's. In those cases where elections in West Bengal have prompted comment from journalists and scholars, attention has been directed almost exclusively to the ways in which electoral politics reflects increasing radicalization of the populace, either by the Communists or by other political forces. Often it is simply observed that the Communist parties have generally done better in West Bengal than they have in the rest of India.

While many reports about the volatility of Bengali politics are exaggerated, there is clearly a sense in which Bengal does exhibit greater political discontinuity than most places. Indeed, it might be argued that the whole of the Bengal region represents a new and very modern political and social phenomenon in the world, if only because of the tragic dilemmas that have resulted from its nightmarish demographic situation. At the present time, for example, there are approximately 48 million people in West Bengal and 75 million people in Bangladesh,[1] making for a combined population of 123 million Bengali speakers living on a piece of land that is only about one and a half times the size of the state of Wisconsin (which has a population of less than five million people). As a number of amateur

---

[1] The Indian Census of 1971 lists 44,440,095 people in West Bengal after a decennial growth rate of 27.2%. More than a million people are added to the state's population each year. The growth rate in Bangladesh is even higher (approximately 3% per annum), and the population there is expected to double in less than 25 years if the present rate continues. For recent analyses see Roger Revelle, "Possible Futures for Bangladesh," *Asia* (New York), Spring 1973, pp. 34-54, and Masihur Rahman Khan, "Bangladesh Population During the First Five-Year Plan Period (1972-77) : A Guestimate," Bangladesh Institute of Development Economics, October 1972 (New Series No. 6).

statisticians have pointed out, Bengal is now more crowded than the United States would be if all of the people of the entire world were placed within the borders of the United States. Yet the population boom in Bengal has barely started. Since half of the Bengali population is now less than 16 years of age, an increasing number of Bengalis will be entering reproductive age groups at alarming rates in the next 16 years, regardless of success or failure in the attempt to reduce birth rates, and the attempt to reduce birth rates has been even less effective in Bengal than it has been in the rest of India.

Overcrowded conditions and their consequences would be sufficient by themselves to produce severe political and social tensions, perhaps like those found in Java, the only area of any size that exhibits man-land ratios comparable to those in Bengal. But at least two other factors that are not generally present elsewhere in Asia have contributed to social disruptions. First, because of the close involvement of Bengal with both the British Raj and the nationalist movement, levels of political conscious-ness and sophistication are generally higher there than elsewhere. Second, Bengal has experienced a decline in almost all areas of life—political, social, economic, and cultural—to the point where Bengali history books now speak of the nineteenth century as the high point of a golden Bengali age and the mid-twentieth century as the nadir of the darkest era. In the words of a *Statesman* editorial written in June 1950, "They [the Bengalis] are con-stantly aware ... of past glories and present potentialities. They do not forget either that Calcutta was long the country's capital or that Bengalis took the lead in the freedom movement. Once they swayed the destinies of India; now they cannot even determine their own."[2]

Overcrowded conditions, high levels of politicization, and intense feelings of relative deprivation have produced a wide variety of radical political movements in Bengal that have occasionally captured the imagina-tion of journalists, while the conditions themselves have frequently appalled world public opinion and discouraged even the most ardent development enthusiasts. Stereotypes of Bengal—as an "international basket case," for example—are further encouraged by the selectivity of the news media, which usually choose to publish or broadcast only those stories about Bengal that concern such massive human tragedies as floods, cyclones, famines, political rioting or murder, and large-scale refugee movements. Little wonder, then, that most people in the world associate the words Calcutta and Bengal with the ultimate in poverty, extremes of human degradation, and an unreserved penchant for radical political movements.

Unfortunately, stereotypes about Bengal serve to mask a most fascinating

---

[2] Quoted in John Broomfield, *Elite Conflict in a Plural Society: Twentieth-Century Bengal* (Berkeley: University of California Press, 1968), p. xviii.

political and social situation that has as yet received little attention from social scientists. For unlike most other places in Asia where widespread protest exists, West Bengal has been deeply involved in an electoral process. Moreover, the electoral involvement of West Bengal's radical political parties is not simply a "camouflage" or a part-time activity designed to conceal more sinister conspiratorial games, but is instead the central concern of most of the leaders and members of these parties. Indeed, electoral politics has increasingly captured the attention of more and more leaders of the state's radical parties, to such an extent that many observers now consider these parties as little more than participants in electoral contests.[3]

In a sense, the radical parties of West Bengal have had little alternative but to become involved in elections. Extreme segmentation in Indian political life has made it impossible for these parties to link mass movements in one linguistic region with political movements in others. Nor has Bengal's radical political leadership been able to overcome the hierarchical aspects of Indian social life, which dictate against truly "mass" movements. Moreover, the toughness of India's national leadership, when coupled with India's military and security preoccupations and the relative isolation of Bengal from the rest of the world, has dealt a death-blow to those attempts by Bengalis to launch guerrilla activities. Having suffered in jail for their several attempts to maintain insurrectionist movements in the subcontinent, the present leadership of Bengal's radical parties has now taken to elections in its attempt to win political power.[4]

Consequently, electoral politics has become more salient in West Bengal than is usually the case, and more important for political parties there than for radical parties elsewhere. Political life in Bengal is also far more complex than stereotypes would allow. This study represents an attempt to unravel some of West Bengal's complexity by examining electoral data for the two major radical political parties in the state. In this way we hope not only to gain some greater insight into the politics of West Bengal, but also, to the extent that it is possible to collect and present data in comparative terms, to offer some concepts and measures that may be relevant to other parts of India and the world.

For purposes of comparative perspective, it is especially important to note that West Bengal exhibits a number of similarities with the rest of India,

---

[3] The notable exception to this tendency for radical parties to become part of the democratic process in West Bengal is the Communist Party of India (Marxist-Leninist), a group of youthful militants which splintered from the CPM (Communist Party of India-Marxist) in 1969 and which itself is now quite factionalized, although still firm in its refusal to engage in electoral politics. On the other hand, it is reported that numerous CPML cadres and others prone to CPML appeals were recruited into the Congress' election drive in 1972.

[4] For an elaboration of these themes see Marcus F. Franda, *Radical Politics in West Bengal* (Cambridge: MIT Press, 1971).

at least insofar as electoral politics is concerned. In West Bengal, as in most other parts of India, the Congress Party dominated electoral politics from 1952 until 1967, winning approximately 40-45% of the popular vote and 60-70% of the seats in the state legislative assembly in the first three national elections. In West Bengal, as elsewhere, Congress faced a number of serious challenges from coalitions of opposition parties between 1967 and 1972, when Mrs. Gandhi's New Congress was returned with a massive majority of seats in the state legislative assembly. In West Bengal, as in other Indian states, the Congress has continually been faced with a host of opposition parties and highly competitive situations in most constituencies, while electoral behaviour has been impressively stable, a large proportion of voters supporting the party of their choice with considerable regularity. As is the case in the rest of India, only more so, the number of voters casting ballots for non-party candidates has shown a marked decline in West Bengal, and the number of independent candidates has also fallen off rather steadily. In West Bengal, as in most areas of India, regional and sub-regional political parties have persisted; voter participation has tended to expand with each election; and alliances among non-Congress parties have increasingly threatened the dominance of the Congress in electoral contests.

In many ways, of course, West Bengal differs from other Indian states, even if the differences are often exaggerated. The principal electoral opposition to the Congress in West Bengal has come from Communist and Marxist-left parties which believe in the legitimacy and efficacy of militant movements and demonstrations, sometimes violent; and some members of these parties participate in electoral contests only to enhance their ability to disrupt the electoral and parliamentary arrangements that have been established in India.[5] Movements of this kind exist in other Indian states as well—indeed, they exist in all electoral democracies—but the intensity and duration of West Bengal's radical movements are somewhat unusual. For purposes of electoral analysis, however, it is important to note that this has not affected the willingness of the Communists to band with other parties toward the end of defeating the Congress in state elections, a phenomenon common to all of India. With the exception of Tamil Nadu, where the Dravida Munetra Kazagham has managed to aggregate most of the votes in opposition to the Congress, all other Indian states have witnessed non-Congress coalition-building among a variety of disparate parties.

Perhaps the principal difference between West Bengal and the majority of other Indian states in recent years is that West Bengal was chronically unstable between 1967 and 1972, a five-year period that witnessed the comings and goings of two Communist-led coalitions, two non-Communist

---

[5] An excellent discussion of Communist party strategies in India appears in Bhabani Sen Gupta, *Communism in Indian Politics* (New York: Columbia University Press, 1972).

coalitions, and three periods of President's Rule (see Figure 1). It was during this five-year period that both urban and rural violence reached a high-point in West Bengal, political paralysis gripped the state, and special elections had to be called (in 1969 and 1971). It is also this turbulent five-year period, however, which offers special possibilities for analysis, not only because it resulted in the unusual situation where four state assembly elections were held (in 1967, 1969, 1971, and 1972) on the basis of a single constituency delimitation, but also because it telescoped into a fairly short period a number of party shifts and alliances (see Figure 2). By studying some of these shifts and alliances on the basis of available electoral data, we hope to be able to gain a greater understanding of the political process in West Bengal than would otherwise be possible, and perhaps to suggest ways in which other Indian states might be studied.

FIGURE 1

Successive Governments in West Bengal (1967-1974)

Dates	Government	Leadership
March 1967-November 1967	First United Front	CPM, CPI, Bangla Congress
November 1967-January 1968	P. C. Ghosh Ministry	Congresss
January 1968-February 1969	President's Rule	Governor appointed by Central Government
February 1969-April 1970	Second United Front	CPM, CPI, Bangla Congress
April 1970-March 1971	President's Rule	Governor appointed by Central Government
March 1971-April 1971	Congress Coalition	Congress, Bangla Congress
April 1971-March 1972	President's Rule	Governor appointed by Central Government
March 1972-present	Congress	Congress

The period under review (from 1967 to the present, with the 1962 elections serving as a point of departure) might be said to have begun in 1964, when the previously united Communist movement in the state split into two competing parties: the established Communist Party of India (CPI) and the splinter Communist Party of India-Marxist, conventionally known as the CPM. This is a period in which Communists made spectacular electoral gains and, for the first time, played an influential role in the state government. Shocked by defeats in 1967 and 1969, the once mighty Congress itself split in two (in late 1969), only to stage a come-back under Mrs. Gandhi's vigorous leadership in the 1972 elections. From a situation of virtual one-party dominance in 1962, West Bengal progressed (or declined) into a fragmented party system, which only recently has shown signs of crystallizing into something suggestive of a two-party or two-party dominant

Figure 2

COMMUNIST ELECTORAL ALLIANCES IN WEST BENGAL (1967-1972)

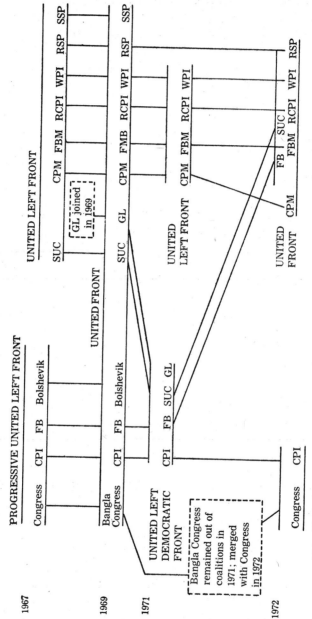

Note: The Bolshevik Party did not join coalitions in 1971 or 1972 nor did the Gurkha League in 1972. The SSP merged with the PSP to form the Socialist Party in 1972 independent of coalition arrangements.

Legend: CPI = Communist Party of India, CPM = Communist Party of India-Marxist, FB = Forward Bloc, FBM = Forward Bloc-Marxist, GL = Gurkha League, PSP = Praja Socialist Party, RCPI = Revolutionary Communist Party of India, RSP = Revolutionary Socialist Party, SSP = Samyukta Socialist Party, SUC = Socialist Unity Centre, WPI = Workers' Party of India.

system. The CPM has become one of the polarities, with Congress the other, and the CPI has exhibited its ability to act as a potential swing group should no other party win a majority of seats in the state legislative assembly.

These are generalizations that are not readily visible from a mere surface reading of election results, if only because of the plethora of political parties that contest in West Bengal and the rapidly shifting fortunes (in terms of seats won) of any given political party. As is indicated in Table 1, the number of seats won by a political party in West Bengal does not correspond in any regular manner with the percentage of votes that the party attracts in an election. For example, the Congress won a solid 40.4% of the votes polled in the assembly elections of 1969 but could garner only 55 of 280 seats, while the CPM in the same elections gained 80 seats with only 19.6% of the total vote. Similarly, in 1972 the CPM could gain only 14 seats with 27.5% of the total vote, while Congress secured a whopping 216 seats with 49.1% of the vote. Such things as party coalitions, margins of victory in individual constituencies, the number of candidates and parties contesting, and a host of other variables play a major role in determining the outcome of elections in West Bengal and other Indian states; and it is some combination of such variables that ultimately explains why a party wins or loses a particular election. Given our present state of research on Indian elections, we are not in a position to assign precise weights to a limited set of variables, or even to identify with any authority which variables are most crucial. However, what we can hope to do is to make a preliminary thrust toward this end.

Our manner of proceeding is as follows. Section II provides a general overview of Communist party presence and performance in West Bengal, tracing out the location and frequency of constituencies contested by the two Communist parties (CP's) and, in general, comparing the extent of Communist electoral gains with those of the Congress Party. Section III is a more detailed attempt to explore the extent to which the CP's have dependable support in various constituencies over time, again in comparison with the Congress. Since our analysis in these two sections points to electoral alliance-building as the key factor in determining election outcomes, we try to analyze three different alliance situations in Section IV : 1) the pattern exhibited in 1967 and 1971, when the two CP's were in direct competition with one another but neither was in alliance with the Congress; 2) the United Front experience of 1969, when the two CP's were in a coalition with one another and with almost all other parties in the state in opposition to the Congress; and 3) the 1972 elections, when the CPI chose to ally with the Congress against the CPM. A brief concluding section summarizes our findings, and in a lengthy appendix we document the distribution of the vote in elections held between 1952 and 1972 for every constituency in the state.

TABLE 1

Votes Polled and Seats Won in West Bengal Legislative Assembly Elections (1962-1972)

	1962		1967		1969		1971		1972	
	% Votes	Seats	% Votes	Seats	% Votes	Seats	% Votes	Seats	% Votes	Seats
Congress	47.3	157	41.1	127	40.4	55	29.8	105	49.1	216
Old Congress	(split from Congress in 1969-70)						5.9	2	1.4	2
Bangla Congress	(founded, 1966)		10.4	34	8.0	33	5.5	5	(merged with Congress)	
PSP	5.0	5	1.9	7	1.3	5	0.6	3	(merged with SSP)	
SSP	(founded, 1964)		2.1	7	1.8	9	0.5	1	(merged with PSP)	
Socialist Party	(founded 1972, result of PSP-SSP merger in that year)								0.9	0
CPI	25.0	50	6.5	16	6.8	30	8.7	13	8.4	35
CPM	(split in 1964)		18.1	43	19.6	80	33.8	113	27.5	14
Forward Bloc	4.6	13	3.9	13	5.4	21	3.7	3	2.7	0
Forward Bloc (M)	0.3	0	0.2	1	0.2	1	0.2	2	0.2	0
SUC	0.7	0	0.7	4	1.5	7	2.1	7	1.4	1
RSP	2.6	9	2.1	6	2.8	12	2.2	3	2.0	3
RCPI	0.4	0	0.3	0	0.4	2	0.4	2	0.2	0
Workers' Party	0.3	0	0.3	2	0.4	2	0.2	2	0.2	1
Jana Sangh	0.5	0	1.3	1	0.8	0	0.3	1	0.2	0
Swatantra	0.6	0	0.8	1	0.1	0	0.1	0	0.0	0
Lok Sevak Sangh	0.7	4	0.7	5	0.7	4	0.6	0	0.4	0
Gurkha League	0.4	2	0.5	2	0.5	4	0.3	2	0.5	0
Other Parties and Independents	11.6	12	9.1	11	9.3	15	5.1	15	4.9	8
Totals	100.0	252	100.0	280	100.0	280	100.0	279*	100.0	280

* In the February 1971 elections, three contests had to be postponed because of the deaths of candidates. Two of these contests were held later in the year and we have included their results in the totals above.

Source : Franda, *Radical Politics in West Bengal*, pp. 116, 118, 274 ; and Paul R. Brass and Marcus F. Franda (eds.), *Radical Politics in South Asia* (Cambridge: MIT Press, 1973), p. 191.

II. An Overview of Communist Presence and Performance in West Bengal Elections

Perhaps the most striking feature of the Communist electoral effort in West Bengal is how limited it has been. When one considers that Communists have twice formed the nucleus of coalition Governments in the state and that the Communist Party of India-Marxist (CPM) was the largest party in the West Bengal legislative assembly in 1969 and 1971, it is instructive to note that at no time prior to 1971 had Communist candidates contested even three-fifths of the seats available to them. The prominence of the Communist movement, electorally at least, has been built from a rather restricted base.

From the First General Elections in 1952 through the Third General Elections in 1962 the Communist Party of India (CPI), united during this period, demonstrated a modest expansion of its electoral ambitions, offering candidates in 36%, 41%, and 58% of the constituencies respectively. Moreover, it secured a higher proportion of the total vote in the state with each election and won an increasing number of seats in the legislative assembly (see Table 2). Even so, by 1962 the CPI was neither a very large party nor an especially potent one. Although it did secure an impressive average vote of 40% in the constituencies which it contested in 1962, it contested only 145 of the 252 constituencies (58%) in the state at that time, of which it won 50 (20%) while receiving one vote out of every four cast in the state as a whole. All this made the CPI the second largest party in West Bengal, but it remained dwarfed by Congress, which in 1962 contested every seat, won 157 of them (62%), and received almost half of the total vote.

There followed a period of judicious contraction, necessitated first by the split in the Communist movement in 1964, then by a feeling-out process in the Fourth General Elections in 1967.[6] Since the 1967 election results revealed weaknesses for both the CPI and CPM, particularly when they contested against one another, the two parties agreed to an elaborate 13-party United Front coalition against Congress in the mid-term elections of 1969, and this in turn enabled the CP's to withdraw from constituencies where they had done badly two years earlier.[7] In the 1969 elections the

---

[6] On the basis of the 1966 delimitation it would appear that 34 constituencies were simply abandoned by the two CP's in the wake of their split. In 1967 the CPM entered 135 constituencies, less than half (48%) of the 280 constituencies in the state. The now smaller CPI put up candidates in only 62 constituencies (22%). However, since the two parties contested the same seats on 38 occasions, one or the other of them was then present in only 159 constituencies (57%). An analysis of CPI-CPM electoral competition appears in Section IV below.

[7] A review of the calculations and maneuverings which produced the United Front in 1969 may be found in Marcus F. Franda, "Electoral Politics in West Bengal: The Growth of the United Front," *Pacific Affairs*, Fall 1969 (Vol. 42), pp. 279-293. The electoral significance of the Front is assessed in Section IV below.

TABLE 2

Communist Presence and Performance in West Bengal Elections: A Summary Overview

	1952	1957	1962	1967		1969		1971		1972	
				CPM	CPI	CPM	CPI	CPM	CPI	CPM	CPI
Number of Constituencies ..	250	252	252	280		280		279a		280	
Seats Contested	89 (36%)	104 (41%)	145 (58%)	135 (48%)	62 (22%)	97 (34%)	36 (12%)	238 (85%)	112 (40%)	208 (74%)	41 (15%)
Seats Won	28 (11%)	46 (18%)	50 (20%)	43 (15%)	16 (6%)	80 (29%)	30 (11%)	113 (40%)	13 (5%)	14 (5%)	35 (13%)
Average Vote,b Entire State	10%	18%	25%	18%	7%	20%	7%	31%	8%	27%	8%

a In three constituencies in 1971 elections were postponed because of the deaths of candidates. We have included figures for the two elections that were held later in the year (in the third of these constituencies elections were not held until 1972).

b Calculated as the average percent vote in each constituency.

two parties together put up candidates in only 47% of the state's constituencies, fewer than the CPM alone had previously.[8]

In spite of this phased contraction, indeed in part because of it, the Communists in 1967 and 1969 improved on their previous performance as a united party. They continued to receive a quarter of the valid votes cast (the lion's share going to the CPM), but they won a larger number of seats in both 1967 and 1969 and entered the state Government on both occasions. Yet it is important to note that in 1969, at the height of Communist success at the polls up to that point, when the CPM won 80 seats to become the largest party in the legislative assembly and the CPI won another 30 seats, the two CP's combined contested less than half of the constituencies in the state.

In 1971 both CP's embarked on a major expansion of their electoral efforts in West Bengal. With the United Front in ruins, each party was obliged to fend pretty much for itself, and competition between the two Communist parties was both bitter and intense. Moreover, the division in Congress ranks promised spectacular new gains for any party capable of taking advantage of the situation. Congress had been humiliated in 1969 by the coalition against it; now Congress had itself split in two, each side putting up candidates against the other and in the process threatening to divide the dependable vote received in the past.

This combination of necessity, opportunity, and competition produced a unique situation in which, for the first time, Communist candidates virtually blanketed the state, contesting 91% of the seats. The CPM alone sponsored candidates in 238 constituencies (85%) in 1971, up from 97 (36%) two years before. It re-entered every constituency where it had been present in 1969 and 132 of the 135 it had contested in 1967. More important, the CPM moved into 104 new constituencies in 1971 and became a major competitor in every district of the state. The CPI also moved boldly into new areas. Having contested only 62 seats in 1967 and 36 in 1969, the CPI was on the ballot in 112 constituencies in 1971, 60 for the first time.[9]

Unfortunately for the CPI, its extended efforts in 1971 failed to pay off. Its share of the vote did not improve—in constituencies contested it actually declined seriously—and the number of seats it won (13) fell to a level lower than in 1967. The CPM, on the other hand, made impressive new gains in 1971. It secured almost a third of the votes tabulated and won an inspiring 113 seats, 33 more than in 1969 and 40% of the total in the state.

---

[8] In 1969 the CPM withdrew from 40 constituencies and the CPI withdrew from 31 (half the number it had contested in 1967). The CPM entered two new constituencies; the CPI entered five.

[9] In 95 of these 112 constituencies the CPI faced the CPM. We shall see that this had a profound impact on the CPI's performance in 1971.

Only a coalition against it prevented the CPM from attempting to form a Government after this, its greatest success in the electoral politics of West Bengal.

In contrast to 1971, the elections of 1972 can be viewed as a time when both CP's again contracted their electoral efforts, also in response to a new electoral situation (in 1972 the CPM ran with few allies; the CPI was allied with Congress). Only a few new forays were made into previously uncontested constituencies. In 1972 the CPM offered candidates in only 14 constituencies it had not entered before, while dropping out of 47 constituencies (of the 47, it had contested 39 of them only once and almost all of these in 1971). The CPI entered only seven new constituencies in 1972 while dropping its candidates in 93 constituencies previously contested (64 of the 93 having been contested only once). In contrast to the 1971 elections, however, the CPI made more gains with its electoral placement in 1972 than did the CPM. Of the seven new constituencies entered by the CPI in 1972, the CPI candidate was successful in six instances, and of the 64 constituencies dropped by the CPI in 1972 none had ever been won by the party. The CPM, on the other hand, won none of the 14 new constituencies it entered in 1972, and it dropped four constituencies that it had won in 1971.

Even the 1971 and 1972 figures, however, give a somewhat inflated notion of the electoral presence of the Communists. Many of the constituencies where the Communists did put up candidates in these latter elections were contested on a "one-time only" basis, and in at least some of them party leaders have given scant attention to building competitive strength. In a multi-party system in which more than 50 political parties have contested elections since 1952, all political parties can be expected to compete in a number of constituencies for reasons other than electoral victory, and the Communists have been no exception in this regard. The Communist parties have at times run candidates as "spoilers" (i.e., to draw votes from other party candidates so that a Communist ally might win or a Communist enemy lose); the CP's, like other parties, have occasionally offered candidates in previously untried constituencies to test the effect of experimental appeals to voters; and both CP's have run candidates in areas where they have had little or no hope of winning the election, in an effort to build or maintain a small party organization that could later be used for more militant activities.

While it would be all but impossible to divine the motivation of the CP's when they contest particular constituencies, greater understanding of Communist electoral presence can be gained by calculating the extent to which the two parties have been on the ballot in a variety of constituencies over time. If a CP has contested a seat in all four elections since 1967, we may consider that constituency to be of central or "core" interest to it. Constituencies contested three times would seem to be of "substantive concern" for the CP in question, especially since every constituency contested three times by one of the Communist parties was contested as recently as 1971, usually after the party had yielded it to an ally in the large United Front of 1969. (In other words, each CP remains active in these "substantive concern" constituencies. None of them has been discarded.) Constituencies contested only once or twice might be labeled peripheral except for the fact that most of them were newly entered in the 1971 elections. They are perhaps more appropriately thought of as constituencies of recent expansion in which the CP's have a new interest. Even so, when one classifies according to a party's presence over four elections, constituencies contested only once or twice are clearly of less significance than those we have identified as being of "core" and "substantive concern." Finally, there are constituencies that the CP's have not contested at all during this period.

As Table 3 indicates, there are a great many constituencies in West Bengal which the CP's have contested either sporadically or not at all. Despite its expanded efforts in 1971, the post-split CPI has never been present in more than half of the constituencies (146 of 280) in the state, and has contested fewer than a sixth (39 of 280) of the seats in the state legislative assembly more than twice. The CPM's record is more impressive. Even so, the number of constituencies which the CPM has contested more than twice amounts to less than half of the total (127 of 280), while "core constituencies" for the CPM constitute barely a third (34%) of the total in the state. By contrast, the Congress has contested 95% of the constituencies more than twice, and almost three-quarters of the constituencies of West Bengal can be considered core constituencies for Congress.

The Communist electoral effort in West Bengal has not only been limited in terms of numbers, it has also been limited geographically. One interesting feature of the split in the movement in 1964 is that it was largely segmental, with one party or the other in effect taking over the position established by the united CPI in different parts of the state. As is indicated in Figure 3, the CPM inherited the party organization in much of the Bengali urban conurbation comprising Burdwan, Nadia, Hooghly, and Howrah districts plus the Calcutta metropolitan area. This is also the region in which it has been most successful. The CPI (see Figure 4) managed to hold on to a good deal of the Communist strength that had previously been built along the south-eastern perimeter of West Bengal, especially Midnapore and that portion of 24-Parganas bordering on Bangladesh. The CPM has been fairly active in the five border districts of northern Bengal, although not with great electoral success. The three districts which have received the least Communist attention over the years are Purulia, Birbhum, and Murshidabad, although the CPM moved conspicuously into all three in

1971 with impressive, if short-lived success.[10]

TABLE 3

Magnitude of Communist Party and Congress Presence in West Bengal Elections (1967-1972)

	CPM	CPI	Congress
Constituencies contested in all four elections	94 (34%)	15 (5%)	208 (74%)
Constituencies contested in three of the four elections	33 (12%)	24 (9%)	57 (20%)
Constituencies contested in two of the four elections	75 (27%)	24 (9%)	15 (5%)
Constituencies contested in one of the four elections	53 (19%)	71 (25%)	—
Constituencies not contested in any of the four elections	25 (9%)	146 (52%)	—
Totals ..	280 (101%)*	280 (100%)	280 (99%)*

* Percentages do not add to 100 because of rounding.

COMMUNIST ELECTORAL PERFORMANCE

It is somewhat difficult to discuss the performance of the CPI and CPM in the aftermath of the 1972 elections, partly because of the extreme disproportions between seats won and percentage of the vote secured by the two CP's (as well as by the Congress), partly because of the frequent charges by the CPM that many of the constituency results in 1972 were heavily influenced by corrupt practices on the part of the Congress organization.   From the very beginning of the 1972 campaign, the CPM charged that Congress Party youth and student wings in West Bengal had collaborated with hired thugs to "let loose a reign of unbridled terror and physical attacks" against CPM candidates and supporters, which made it impossible for the CPM and its allies to conduct a normal election campaign.   Moreover, the CPM State Committee issued a statement in which it alleged that the Election Commission had "removed thousands of names of genuine voters from the electoral rolls with the specific objective of helping the ruling party," while "thousands of fake names were added to pad the electoral rolls."   In a memorandum to Mrs. Gandhi in late January, the leader of

---

[10] In 1971 the CPM won 16 of 36 seats in Purulia, Birbhum, and Murshidabad. A year later it lost every seat contested in these districts.

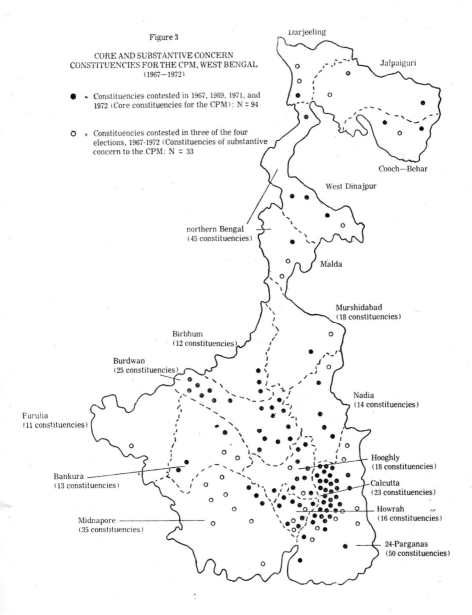

Figure 3

CORE AND SUBSTANTIVE CONCERN
CONSTITUENCIES FOR THE CPM, WEST BENGAL
(1967—1972)

● ₊ Constituencies contested in 1967, 1969, 1971, and
1972 (Core constituencies for the CPM): N = 94

○ ₒ Constituencies contested in three of the four
elections, 1967-1972 (Constituencies of substantive
concern to the CPM: N = 33

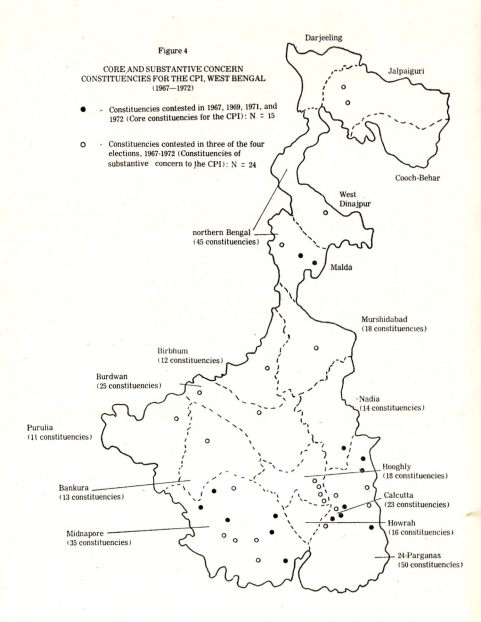

Figure 4

CORE AND SUBSTANTIVE CONCERN
CONSTITUENCIES FOR THE CPI, WEST BENGAL
(1967—1972)

● - Constituencies contested in 1967, 1969, 1971, and
1972 (Core constituencies for the CPI): N = 15

○ - Constituencies contested in three of the four
elections, 1967-1972 (Constituencies of
substantive concern to the CPI): N = 24

the West Bengal CPM electoral organization, Mr. Jyoti Basu, listed 34 West Bengal assembly constituencies where "free and fair elections had been seriously endangered" as a result of "violent operations by Congress hoodlums and the police." Continuing further, the memorandum stated:

> Hoodlums operate almost in all cases with the knowledge of the local police and with their active help. In every case where rowdies are confronted by the local police, the police actively intervene to beat up and arrest those who defend themselves. There are cases where Congress hoodlums dragged people out of their homes, beat them and then handed them over to the police. But the police, instead of apprehending the Congress supporters for taking law into their hands, arrest their victims.[11]

In its last issue before the March 1972 elections, *People's Democracy* (the CPM weekly) stated that 487 CPM organizers and supporters had been killed in West Bengal since the downfall of the last CPM-led ministry on March 16, 1970, the names of which had all been listed in previous issues of the newspaper. Moreover, the party called for an 11-point programme to "restore social and political peace in West Bengal," which included demands for freedom of assembly, assurances against indiscriminate arrest, release of political prisoners detained without trial, and withdrawal of the Central Reserve Police from West Bengal. At the same time, however, CPM leaders indicated that they did not expect their demands to be met, nor did they expect the campaign of violence against the CPM to stop since, in Jyoti Basu's words, the CPM had become the object of a "conspiracy at the top."[12]

In response to these charges, Congress Prime Minister Indira Gandhi stated that Basu's January memorandum was filled with "blatant lies" and pointed to statistics to show that the incidence of violence in West Bengal had actually declined after the imposition of President's Rule in 1970. Moreover, a number of central government leaders undertook tours of West Bengal to investigate the CPM's allegations, and all issued positive (if qualified) statements attesting to the fairness of the elections and the decrease in violence. The Central Election Commissioner, Mr. S. P. Sen-Verma, for example, found after this tour of the state that the elections in West Bengal were "undoubtedly fair," although he also admitted that "there are pockets of dissidence where normal campaigning has been somewhat circumscribed." Similarly, Mr. K. C. Pant, Union Minister of State for Home Affairs, found that there had been "a striking improvement in the law and order situation in West Bengal," but with the significant exception of "inter-party clashes," which Mr. Pant described as follows: "Very often

---

[11] *Times of India* (New Delhi), February 1, 1972, p. 20.

[12] *Hindustan Times* (New Delhi), February 1, 1972, p. 20.

the case is the CPM's resistance in its strongholds to the entry of Cong-ressmen or the CPM's bid to dislodge Congress members." The Union Home Secretary, Mr. Govind Narain, also found that violent political inci-dents in West Bengal had declined—from 646 in the month of July 1971 to only 92 in January 1972— while political murders had declined from 125 in July of 1971 to only 17 in January 1972.[13]

From the standpoint of the central government, no one was willing to argue that the 1972 elections in West Bengal were held in an atmosphere of complete calm; but in light of the state's recent political history, many observers were surprised that the elections could be held without greater violence and disruption than what undoubtedly took place. Even politi-cians in West Bengal—of all political suasions—were ready to admit that "some Congress youth may have ganged up on the CPM with the assistance of antisocial elements," but those opposed to the CPM were quick to point out that the situation in 1972 was much better than in 1971, when elections in three West Bengal constituencies had to be postponed because of the violent deaths of actual candidates. In the words of a *Statesman* editorial of March 3, 1972:

> The claim by West Bengal's Inspector-General of Police that the law and order situation in the State is "normal".... tends to confirm the Chief Election Commissioner's view, expressed late last month, that the State is in this respect "definitely" in a better condition than it was last year. Much would of course depend on what is conceived to be "normal" and too strict an application of this concept would almost certainly be misleading in West Bengal's conditions....

Moreover, most observers in India could muster little sympathy for the CPM in West Bengal, since it was patently clear to everyone that the CPM itself had been more responsible than any other party for the rapid increase in violent activities after 1967. To quote Mr. N. C. Menon, a correspondent for the *Hindustan Times* in New Delhi, writing on February 26, 1972:

> If the CPM now complains that they are unable even to enter some of the constituencies, there is undeniably some truth in the charge, but the party is only reaping the whirlwind of violence they themselves have sown.

In short, the allegations of the CPM that the 1972 elections in West Bengal were not free and fair throw into bold relief the dilemma that all democratic societies face when trying to allow normal freedoms to a political party that is committed to the use of violence. To refuse to use the police and the army to control organized violence is to invite even greater dis-ruption, to the point where a democratic process becomes impossible. But

---

[13] *Ibid.*, February 6 1972, p. 21.

by using the police and the army against those who claim to use violence legitimately, a democratic government always leaves itself open to the charge that it is discriminating against particular opposition parties. What is striking about the 1972 elections in this context was the willingness and ability of the Congress Party in West Bengal to counter effectively the violent tactics initiated by the CPM, in sharp contrast to previous indecision on the part of the Congress organization.

Widespread charges of corruption create special problems for politicians and government leaders, of course, but they perhaps create even more problems for the electorally minded social scientist. Are we simply to disregard the 1972 state elections in West Bengal because of the intensity and frequency of corruption charges in these as compared to prior elections? Are we to discount the results of the elections in some constituencies (for example, in the 34 constituencies mentioned in the Basu memorandum) and, if so, to what extent do we discount them?

After considering a number of alternative strategies, we have decided simply to take the results of the 1972 elections at their face value, for at least three compelling reasons. First, it is plausible that the 1972 elections were as fair as any previous elections in West Bengal, and that CPM charges of electoral "rigging" were merely devised as a tactical ploy to be used in post-election campaigns against the Congress. Second, most independent observers of Bengali politics are convinced that any electoral "rigging" engaged in by the Congress in 1972 was of only marginal significance in determining the electoral outcome, since it was clear that the Congress-CPI alliance was the overwhelming favourite of the electorate in any case. Finally, the official election results for 1972 indicate that, with some few exceptions (primarily in Burdwan District) the CPM, CPI, and Congress vote totals—as well as the vote totals of other parties—exhibit a remarkable continuity between previous elections and the 1972 contest, to such an extent that one would have to conclude that the effects of any "rigging" that took place in 1972 would not be severely damaging to analysis.

Regardless of one's view of the fairness of the 1972 elections, however, what is striking about the vote figures themselves is the way in which they establish the CPM as a very strong and relatively independent state electoral party, despite the fact that the CPM fared so badly in terms of seats won. For example, even though the CPM won only 14 of the 208 seats it contested in 1972, the party secured an average vote of 38.9% in its 94 core constituencies, 36.7% on the average in its 32 constituencies of substantive concern, an average 33.7% of the vote in the 68 constituencies it was contesting for the second time since 1962, and an average 27.4% of the vote in the 14 constituencies it entered for the first time in 1972.[14] Moreover, the CPM

---

[14] One might conclude from these figures that the CPM tends to receive a larger vote the

lost only 10 of its security deposits in 1972, a very small number in comparison to most Indian political parties. Stated somewhat differently, the CPM secured an average vote of 36.1% in the 208 constituencies that it contested —a very high average for Indian political parties, comparable only to the average vote of Congress and the major state parties—and it finished second in 185 constituencies in 1972, a whopping 74% of the total it contested and a solid two-thirds of the constituencies in the state as a whole.

In comparison to the CPM, the CPI in 1972 contested only 41 constituencies, winning a startling 35 of these, finishing second in four contests and third in only two constituencies, while averaging 54.3% of the vote in those 41 constituencies in which it entered candidates. However, unlike the CPM, the CPI is not the kind of party which can stand very effectively on its own, as was demonstrated most clearly in the 1971 elections. Since the party split in 1964, the CPI has never gained more than 8.7% of the vote in any statewide election, and its expansion to many new constituencies in 1971 was a disastrous failure. In order to win an appreciably large number of seats and to have a chance of entering the Government, the CPI needs allies—preferably before rather than after an election. As will be shown later, it was the CPI's electoral alliance with the Congress that was crucial to its success in 1972. At the same time, the CPI is large and strong enough (an average of 20% of the vote in the 112 constituencies it contested in 1971) to be an effective coalition partner for the CPM or for Congress. Barring a total realignment of Bengali political forces, it is likely to occupy a critical swing position in the increasingly polarized politics of West Bengal in the foreseeable future.

Indeed, on the basis of an analysis of a wide variety of factors related to electoral outcomes in different kinds of constituencies, one is led to the conclusion that the most critical determinant of election results in West Bengal in recent years has been the interaction between the Congress, the CPM, and the CPI, the three largest parties in the state. One could even read the oscillations in election outcome as a protest vote against whatever combination of these three forces was in power, lending credence to the suspicion that it does not pay to be "the Government" in West Bengal! At any rate, there is no consistent or clear evidence that there are determinable patterns over time which would relate election results for any of the Bengali parties with such things as (1) levels of voter turnout, (2) the number of candidates contesting, or (3) changes in support for other parties. Nor

---

more it contests a constituency; and indeed, it is true that the presence over time of CPM candidates and cadres has not alienated the voters in the great majority of constituencies. On the other hand, the strong association noted between presence and support is also a reflection of the fact that the CPM, like other parties, has tended to contest more often in constituencies where its support is greatest.

is there evidence that any party in West Bengal has consistently secured more votes in constituencies where a particular rival party provides the leading opposition. Finally, we have found no consistent and clear correlation between the vote totals for any leading party and such demographic variables as rural-urban proportions of the electorate, or the presence of scheduled castes and scheduled tribes.[15] Obviously, each of these factors has played a role in particular constituencies at particular times, and in some cases may have even influenced a given statewide election; but none of them has yet attained statistical significance as an indicator establishing patterns over time.

The overall picture presented by the electoral data for West Bengal, therefore, is one of a party system which is still in considerable flux, with some few patterns seemingly crystallizing over time, but even then not very firmly. The Congress is clearly the most powerful party in the state, having built an organization that can consistently and realistically contest elections in virtually every constituency, obviously being aided by the national Congress organization and blessed with all of the advantages that derive from the possession of national political power. As in other Indian states, Congressmen in West Bengal can continue to maintain themselves even when the party is out of power at the state level, because of their attachments to the national party organization. They can secure funds, they can get jobs and patronage, and they can otherwise gain influence through national contacts. Even so, the Congress has been beaten more than once in West Bengal, largely because of its own internal factionalism but also because of the increasing ability of the CPM to act as an alternative pole around which effective party coalitions can rally.

The CPM, on the other hand, is a smaller electoral party than the Congress in West Bengal, even though it has now attained a position of some preeminence as the leading opposition party in the state. Granted the size of the CPM organization, its continued presence in so many constituencies, and its demonstrated ability to survive independently of electoral coalitions, it is most likely that the CPM will continue to be a major force in the electoral politics of West Bengal for some time to come. This is not to argue, however, that the electoral growth of the CPM can be assumed without question. The CPM has no advantages like those enjoyed by the state Congress Party in its linkages with the central government, but is instead at a disadvantage because of its extremely weak position at the

---

[15] For each election year we made detailed analyses of how Communist and Congress support and the identity of winning candidates were influenced by such variables as turnout, the number and type of candidates contesting, past and present margins of victory, the distribution of the vote, and several sociological and locational characteristics of constituencies. These data are not reported in this study because there was little consistency to the findings.

national level. Not only does the CPM lack the potential patronage of the Congress Party, it is also more vulnerable to opposition charges that it is somehow anti-Indian or in some ways "foreign" to Bengal, if only because of its links to the international Communist movement. This clearly restrains the CPM when delicate regional, communal, or foreign policy issues arise, preventing the party from taking the bold positions adopted by powerful non-Communist state parties like the DMK in Tamil Nadu.

The CPM has other disadvantages too. Its leadership is pervasively upper class, and the party's claim to speak for the downtrodden has consistently been disputed, rhetorically by other parties and electorally by a sizeable majority of the public. Moreover, the CPM still has a very strong factional element that does not believe in the efficacy of electoral contests, and it is this wing of the party that has for years urged a diminished electoral emphasis in overall CPM strategy. At present the non-electoralists in the CPM have persuaded the party to adopt a position of non-participation in electoral contests and a boycott of the state legislative assembly in protest against the allegedly rigged elections of 1972. But this stance presents a number of dilemmas. If the CPM is going to reenter electoral contests at some point, it will certainly have to do so over the objections of some members of its powerful non-electoral wing; and it will have to legitimize its change of posture in the eyes of a politically sophisticated electorate. So long as it remains out of electoral contests and the legislative assembly, however, it will be beset by factionalism of another kind, led by electoralists who want to build an entirely different kind of support for the party than that envisaged by the anti-electoral militant wing.[16] As has been pointed out on a number of occasions, all political parties in West Bengal seem to be plagued by constant factional threats, and party splits are the norm rather than the exception. All bets about future party performance (Communist and Congress alike) have to be hedged to take account of this phenomenon.

It is in this context that the "swing" potential of the CPI assumes even greater importance than might otherwise be the case, since positions taken by the CPI can either help to promote or slow the pace of party factionalism in both Congress and the CPM. Since party factionalism in the West Bengal Congress has now evolved into something resembling a sparring match between a youthful and more radical Congress organization and an older and more established governmental leadership, the CPI could conceivably choose to ally itself with either of the factions, could perhaps act as mediator between the two, or could simply try to stand by as a silent spectator. Similarly, the CPI could either promote or impede

---

[16] For a recent review of factionalism within the CPM see Marcus F. Franda, "Radical Politics in West Bengal," in *Radical Politics in South Asia*, edited by Paul R. Brass and Marcus F. Franda (Cambridge: MIT Press, 1973), pp. 183-219.

factionalism within the CPM: by siding with either of the two major factions, by ignoring factional fighting in rival parties, or by attempting mediation when intra-CPM factional fights occur. In light of its past performance as an electoral party in West Bengal, as well as its close attachments to (including funding from) Moscow, the CPI would certainly be more effective in any of these roles than would other political parties in the state.

But the CPI has problems too. Since it has such a restricted electoral base and is so obviously dependent on allies for a strong electoral showing, it constantly runs the risk of having its party members absorbed or coopted into larger and more powerful electoral organizations. To combat this, the CPI must repeatedly try to stake out for itself independent political positions, an extremely difficult thing to do when a party is so heavily dependent on alliances with others. In this context, perhaps the most worrisome figures for the CPI are those that relate to the electoral fortunes of the smaller Marxist-left parties in West Bengal, all of which have seen their vote total diminish over the years (for example, see the figures for the Forward Bloc in Table 1).

Some idea of the restricted electoral base of the CPI, as compared to the CPM and the Congress, can be gained from Table 4, which details the frequency with which the major parties have been victorious in the same constituencies over time. As is indicated in this table, the CPI has won at least once during the last four elections in 52 different constituencies, as compared with 135 constituencies won at least once by the CPM and 241 by the Congress. Moreover, the CPI has won more than twice in only 12 constituencies, as against 34 for the CPM and 75 for the Congress, while the comparable figures for winning more than once are only 25 for the CPI, 73 for the CPM, and a whopping 164 for the Congress.

These figures become even more meaningful when one looks at their geographical distribution, in the manner of Figures 5 and 6. Figure 5 points out the extent to which the CPM wins frequently primarily in Calcutta and surrounding districts. Indeed, all 34 of the constituencies that the CPM has won more than twice could be said to lie within the Calcutta urban conurbation and industrial grid, stretching from the southern suburbs of Calcutta up through Burdwan to Asansol and Durgapur. Then too, only a third (34 of 101) of the constituencies that the CPM has won once or twice could be said to lie outside of this area.

Similarly, the CPI does best in those areas where it contests frequently (see Figure 6)—i.e., along the southern perimeter of West Bengal and in that portion of 24-Parganas District that borders on what is now Bangladesh. Of the 12 constituencies won by the CPI more than twice, eight of them fall within this area, while three of the others are in Calcutta and the last is in northern Bengal. The restricted base of the CPI is indicated by the

TABLE 4

Frequency of Party Victories in Constituencies won by the Major Parties of West Bengal (1967-1972)

	CPI		CPM		Congress	
Number of constituencies won four times	5	(2%)	8	(3%)	23	(3%)
Number of constituencies won three times	7	(3%)	26	(9%)	52	(19%)
Number of constituencies won twice	13	(5%)	39	(14%)	89	(32%)
Number of constituencies won once	27	(10%)	62	(22%)	77	(28%)
Number of constituencies never won	228	(81%)	145	(52%)	39	(14%)
Totals ..	280	(101%)*	280	(100%)	280	(101%)*

* Percentages do not add to 100 because of rounding.

fact that the CPM is almost as strong in CPI strongholds as is the CPI, while in CPM strongholds the CPI is no match for the larger Communist party. This being the case, the CPI does not really have a regional stronghold in the same sense as the CPM, which means that the CPI is constantly battling for political survival in every part of the state.

III.   Vote Trends and the Dependability of Communist Support

For most observers the drama of the election results in West Bengal over the past decade has been furnished by the rapid rise of the CPM to a position of electoral power and then by the apparent collapse of the CPM in the 1972 elections. This is in sharp contrast to the CPI's failure to expand its support during this same period and seems—not surprisingly —to be conversely related to the fortunes of the Congress Party. The figures that are usually adduced to illustrate these trends are those which show the CPM receiving almost a third of all valid votes cast in the state in 1971, compared with only a fifth of the valid votes in 1969 and just under a fifth in 1967. During this short period the number of seats won by the CPM increased from 43 in 1967 to 80 in 1969 to 113 in 1971, only to fall to a miserable 14 seats in 1972, when the CPM secured a little more than a quarter of the votes cast in the state. During these years the CPI's share of the vote has remained steady at 7-8%, although the number of seats it has won has varied widely, from lows of 13 in 1971 and 16 in 1967 to a high of 35 in 1972.

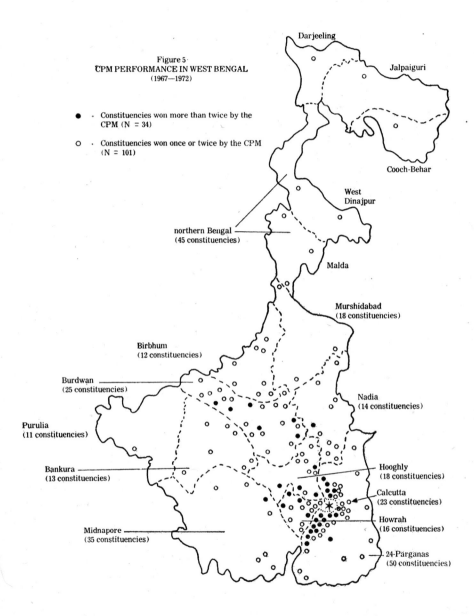

Figure 5
CPM PERFORMANCE IN WEST BENGAL
(1967—1972)

● · Constituencies won more than twice by the
   CPM (N = 34)

○ · Constituencies won once or twice by the CPM
   (N = 101)

Darjeeling

Jalpaiguri

Cooch-Behar

West
Dinajpur

northern Bengal
(45 constituencies)

Malda

Murshidabad
(18 constituencies)

Birbhum
(12 constituencies)

Burdwan
(25 constituencies)

Nadia
(14 constituencies)

Purulia
(11 constituencies)

Hooghly
(18 constituencies)

Bankura
(13 constituencies)

Calcutta
(23 constituencies)

Howrah
(16 constituencies)

Midnapore
(35 constituencies)

24-Parganas
(50 constituencies)

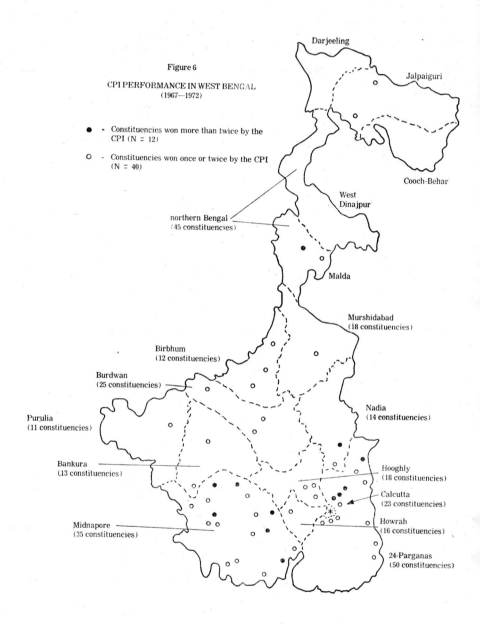

Figure 6

CPI PERFORMANCE IN WEST BENGAL
(1967—1972)

● - Constituencies won more than twice by the
    CPI (N = 12)

○ - Constituencies won once or twice by the CPI
    (N = 40)

Unfortunately, it is difficult to interpret state-level figures such as these when the number of constituencies contested varies so markedly from one election to the next and the nature of party alliances shifts so dramatically. Does a higher proportion of the vote reflect a genuine improvement in the party's standing with the electorate or simply the fact that it had many more candidates running, or perhaps was running with different electoral allies in a substantially different set of constituencies ? To what extent do political parties in West Bengal have a dependable following that can be counted on in election after election, regardless of the number of seats won in any particular year? To what extent are parties able to transfer support to electoral allies from one election to the next? In short, how much continuity or discontinuity is there in Bengali politics over time?

Looking only at constituencies contested in a given election, or even over two successive elections, is of little help in answering questions like these. Figures relating to a party's average vote per constituency are likely to be influenced upward by temporary transfers of support from coalition allies and downward by an expansion of the party's own electoral activity, so that figures for a large number of constituencies in any given election will be either temporarily high or low, depending on the nature of the party's electoral strategy in that year. For example, even though the CPM's share of the statewide vote increased impressively in 1971 and fell somewhat in 1972, its average vote in constituencies contested declined from 54% in 1969 to 37% in 1971 and 36% in 1972, the first of these figures reflecting the impact of CPM involvement in the United Front of 1969. For the most part the CPM contested only its best constituencies in 1969; and in many of these its vote was augmented by support which had previously gone to one or more of its allies (hence its strong showing in terms of average vote per constituency contested in 1969). In 1971 and 1972, however, the CPM expanded into constituencies where its strength was untested, and it also lost the assistance of its electoral allies of 1969, thereby causing a diminution of its average vote per constituency contested in 1971 and 1972. The exact nature of the party's standing with the electorate remains unclear.

One way around this impasse is to control, in effect, for changes in the number of constituencies entered, a method we employed while examining changes in CP strength from one election to the next in different parts of the state. For example, in 1971 the CPI showed a modest improvement in its voter appeal in only two West Bengal districts—Midnapore, the closest thing to a stronghold the CPI has, and neighbouring Bankura.[17]

---

[17] The CPI's share of the vote increased from 15% in 1967 to 17% in 1969 to 20% in 1971 in Midnapore and from 3% to 4% to 10% in Bankura across these same years. Elsewhere the CPI vote changed little or not at all.

However, comparing the number of constituencies contested each year with the average vote received in Midnapore and Bankura in 1971 reveals that actually the CPI position in Midnapore and Bankura had not improved. Its slight increase in total vote secured in 1971 was a function primarily of its contesting more, while in the constituencies contested its average vote had declined sharply.[18]   By contrast, the CPM's total vote improved in every district or region of the state between 1967 and 1971; and when the same test is applied, in only two districts (Purulia and Murshidabad) did the growth in CPM support reflect mere expansion of party effort. Outside of Purulia and Murshidabad the CPM was indeed a stronger party in 1971 than it had been in 1967.

But even these kinds of figures tell us little about the dependable support of a party, and they are of almost no predictive value whatsoever. What we would like to have—ideally, of course—is an approximate measure of the institutionalized or dependable support that a party can muster in a constituency under different electoral circumstances.   How much support can a party count on in a given constituency when it runs on its own ?   To what degree must it depend on allies for an electoral victory ?   What is the lowest total that the party has secured, and under what circumstances does it maximize its chances of winning ?

The principal difficulty standing in the way of an examination of voter appeal in the same constituencies over time is the Indian penchant for redrawing constituency boundaries periodically (usually every ten years or so), which means that it is rare to find a series of elections reflecting the same delimitation.   As mentioned previously, however, one happy consequence of West Bengal's political turmoil since 1967 has been the need to hold elections fairly frequently, so that we now have data for West Bengal over four successive elections (1967, 1969, 1971, and 1972), all of which were conducted on the basis of the same constituency delimitation.   The existence of such data has made it possible for us to construct a set of categories that are useful in exploring questions like those posed above, categories which might be helpful in examining other Indian states where similar data are available.[19]

VOTE TRENDS

In order to understand the ways in which the Communist vote has

---

[18] In Midnapore the CPI averaged 53% of the vote in the ten constituencies it contested in 1967.   Its record in 1969 was almost identical.   But in 1971 the CPI entered 25 Midnapore constituencies, a notable increase, but averaged only 28% of the vote in them, a notable decrease.   The situation in Bankura is similar.

[19] For example, see the study in this series by Robert L. Hardgrave, Jr., "The Communist Parties of Kerala: An Electoral Profile."

changed in the same constituencies over time, we have established four categories reflecting the general trends in party support that might conceivably occur. These categories are constancy, growth, decline, and fluctuation. *Constancy* of performance is defined as variation of no more than 5% over the four elections from the share of the vote received by the party in question when it first contested a constituency.[20] The basic idea of constancy is that the party has acquired the same general magnitude of support in a particular constituency each time it has run, notwithstanding changes in the local competitive configuration.

We label a party's vote trend in a given constituency *growth* when support for the party over time meets one of two conditions: (1) when there has been a linear increase in the party's vote across a number of successive elections exceeding 5% overall or, in the case of constituencies contested twice, an increase of more than 5% in the vote received from the base election to the next one contested; and (2) when there has been "basic growth" in core or substantive concern constituencies despite a minor deviation or two along the way denying linearity.[21] For example, the party may have suffered a slight decline in constituency support in the second of three elections, or in the second and/or third of four elections, but then achieved a notably higher vote in the last election than it had received in the first (for example, 32%-29%-41%, or in the case of four elections, 32%-29%-29%-41%), still exhibiting "basic growth" over time. Or the party's vote may have improved in the second of three elections, or in the second and/or third of four elections, but then dropped off slightly in the fourth (for example, 34%-56%-52%, or in the case of four elections, 34%-56%-58%-53%), yet still reflect a trend of "basic growth." In each case an overall pattern of growth may be discerned, and it can be said that the party has been building support.[22]

---

[20] If the party has contested a constituency in all four or in three of the four elections, the maximum possible disparity between the votes received each time is 10% (for example, 40%-35%-45%). If the party has contested only twice, the maximum difference allowed is 5%. We regard these standards for constant support to be quite stringent, particularly when one takes into account the possibilities for variation in a party's vote in the fluid multi-party situation that has existed in West Bengal and most of India over the past decade.

[21] The difference between a trend of 31%-46%-49% and 31%-49%-46% is rather meaningless. Allowing for basic growth by accepting minor deviations is both less rigid and truer to the trends revealed in the data than is an insistence upon linearity.

[22] Operationally, a deviant decline may not exceed 5% from the previous peak, while the growth demonstrated must be more than 5% above the base-year figure. Needless to say, when the changes from year to year are rather small, the overall pattern of growth becomes somewhat questionable, as in the case of a 40%-46%-41% trend. The differences between categories are bound to seem insignificant the closer the distributions come to the cut-off points. (The example cited is within 1% of qualifying as constancy.) Without excusing the rough edges in our criteria, we do feel that they are sensible, if strict, and that they are eminently serviceable for the distributions we have found in the Communist data.

Situations of *decline* are the reverse of growth. The percentage of the vote received by a party may simply have decreased steadily across a number of elections, in which case we require only that the cumulative loss of support exceed 5% if it is to be described as decline. In the case of constituencies contested twice, a drop of more than 5% from the first to the second election qualifies as decline. A modest complexity appears once again when in core and substantive concern constituencies the overall pattern is one of decline, yet with some variation in direction. We count as "basic decline" situations in which a party does somewhat better in the second of three elections, or in the second and/or third of four elections, so long as the deviation from the first election is no greater than 5% and the party's vote in the last election has dropped to more than 5% below the level achieved in the first election. Similarly, we accept as "basic decline" situations in which the party's support improves in the last election (be it the third or fourth in a series) by within 5% of the second election, after having decreased by more than 5% from the first election.[23]

Our final category of support trends, *fluctuation,* applies only to a party's core and substantive concern constituencies (for its vote to fluctuate the party must have contested a constituency at least three times) and represents a magnitude of inconsistent change in the vote too great for us to claim either basic growth or basic decline. Situations of fluctuation are those in which the vote varies so widely from one election to the next that the trends cannot be classified except by exclusion. The operational key is that a party's share of the vote must vary by more than 5%, but in different directions on different occasions.

Any operationalization of this kind is bound to be somewhat arbitrary. But in settling upon this set of requirements for constancy, growth, decline, and fluctuation we believe we have established a standard which is both admirably suited to a study of the Communists in West Bengal and serviceable to analysis of the CP's and other parties elsewhere—including newer and lesser parties—all over the country and at various points in time, so long as data exist for three or more elections held within the same delimitation. To the extent that we have erred, we hope it is from being too severe. In any event, we are now in a position to classify the overall trend in the Communist vote for every constituency contested more than once, and we can also identify the level of *floor support,* the lowest vote a CP has received in the four elections under review, for each case.

Before turning to the data, however, it might be helpful to furnish a number of examples of these trends in voter appeal that demonstrate the kinds of distinctions we are attempting to make.

---

[23] For example, a vote trend of 40%-42%-27%-29% would be considered decline, as would a trend of 40%-27%-31%-30%. Again, the standards are weak when the controlling change is small. Thus a trend of 40%-34%-39% is unavoidably considered decline.

Examples of Constant Support: Given our criteria, one of the constituencies that we can identify as exhibiting constant support for the CPM is constituency # 65 (Tehatta) in Nadia District, a constituency bordering on what is now Bangladesh that has absorbed a large number of international refugees over the years. The CPM, like most political parties in West Bengal, has made a sustained effort to court the five million or so refugees that came into West Bengal from Pakistan in the 1950's and 1960's, and electoral data would indicate that in the case of Tehatta such efforts have been quite successful. In Tehatta the CPM received a vote of 43% in 1967, 45% in 1969, 46% in 1971, and 40% in 1972, reflecting the CPM's solid base of support—at a fairly high level—in this constituency. Although these figures do indicate that CPM strength in Tehatta increased slightly between 1967 and 1971 and then declined in 1972, the overall change to date—from the base year of 1967—does not exceed 5%, thereby making constancy the appropriate designation. Had the trend been, for example, 43%-45%-49%-48%, we would have been obliged to code the CPM vote in Tehatta as growth; had it been 43%-45%-46%-37%, we would have coded it decline, while a trend of 43%-45%-37%-46% would have been deemed fluctuation.

A second example of constancy, at a rather low floor level, is the case of the vote trend for the CPM in Kalimpong, a constituency (#20) that has been dominated since 1947 by the Congress and the Gurkha League. (The Gurkha League is a small party composed largely of Nepalis, which contests only in the five constituencies of Darjeeling District.) In 1971 and 1972 the CPM attempted to make inroads into Gurkha League strength in Darjeeling District, as part of its general strategy of expanding into new areas. But in the case of Kalimpong constituency, electoral data demonstrate the failure of the CPM to do so. In Kalimpong the CPM received only 16.6% of the vote in 1971 and 12.3% of the vote in 1972, these being the first two elections in which the CPM contested the constituency. We classify this constituency as one exhibiting a vote trend of constancy for the CPM, at a low floor level, since the difference between the figures for the two elections is less than 5%.

Examples of Growth: One constituency in Darjeeling District where the CPM has been successful in displacing the Gurkha League as the largest opposition party is Phansidewa (#24), the constituency in which Naxalbari is located. (Naxalbari is the village in which the "Naxalite" agitations of the late 1960's first took place.) Here the CPM has increased its percentage of the vote over the four elections from 29.3% in 1967 and 28.6% in 1969 to 33.3% in 1971 and 37.7% in 1972. This is clearly growth, although the CPM has not yet won the seat and the reasons for its growth in Phansidewa are the subject of considerable debate, both in the constituency and in the state of West Bengal. Some argue that the CPM has made steady gains here because of the favourable climate for radicalism created by the Naxalbari agitation; some argue that CPM gains have been possible only because the Gurkha League is the only established opposition party in Darjeeling and the League does not have a large Gurkha population to draw on in this particular constituency. Still others contend that the CPM has merely benefited from a series of favourable electoral alignments in Phansidewa.

A second example of growth, which can be explained in a less ambiguous manner, is constituency #171 (Champdani) in Hooghly District, where both the CPI and CPM have been vying for support among peasant-cultivators, in an area where the new technology in agriculture has been introduced over the last decade. But the fact that the CPI has steadily increased its support in Champdani—from 16.3% in 1967 to 21.1% in 1971 to 51.3% in 1972—would seem in this case to be less a function of CPI ability to woo peasant-cultivators as it is simply the result of various alliances the CPI has made in successive elections. In 1967, when it contested against both the CPM and the Congress in Champdani, the CPI secured only a sixth of the vote, prompting it to surrender this seat to the CPM in 1969 without a contest. Then when the CPI reentered the constituency in 1971, it picked up a small amount of support from the Congress, whose vote was steadily declining. When Congress threw its support to the CPI in 1972, the CPI was able to defeat the CPM in Champdani; but one wonders if the CPI can continue to exhibit growth in Champdani (or in a number of constituencies like it) in future electoral contests. According to our criteria, at any rate, Champdani is presently coded as a growth constituency for the CPI, but at the low floor support level of 16.3%.

A final example of growth, in this case for the CPM, is provided by the vote trend exhibited in constituency #179 (Dhaniakali), located just to the west of Calcutta in the industrial belt that stretches from Calcutta through Asansol to Durgapur. In Dhaniakali the CPM secured only 11.7% of the vote in 1967 and then threw its support to the successful Forward Bloc candidate as part of the United Front electoral alliance of 1969. However, during the tenure of the United Front ministry in 1969-70 the CPM pursued particularly aggressive tactics in its attempt to capture the trade unions dominated by its allies in the Front, and one of the places in which it was most successful in this endeavor was Hooghly District. As a result of the CPM's ability to capture Forward Bloc trade unions in Hooghly in 1969-70, the Forward Bloc lost Dhaniakali (and a number of other constituencies) to the CPM in 1971. By 1972, therefore, the Forward Bloc was convinced that it had to throw its support to the Congress Party, with the result that the Congress captured Dhaniakali constituency from the CPM by a margin of 56% to 44% in a straight fight in 1972. In this instance, even though the CPM vote declined by a slight margin between

1971 and 1972, we have coded Dhaniakali as a growth constituency for the CPM, since its percentage of the vote increased from 11.7% in 1967 to 46.4% in 1971 and then declined by less than 5%, to 44% in 1972. Had the CPM vote declined to less than 41.4% in Dhaniakali in 1972, we would have coded the trend as fluctuation.

Examples of Decline: An example of basic decline in support for the CPM is Kaliaganj, constituency #29 in West Dinajpur District, where a popular Congress candidate (Debendranath Roy) and a hard-working Congress organization have made life difficult for the opposition in recent years. The CPM came close to challenging the Congress in Kaliaganj in 1967, when it secured 39.8% of the vote against 42.1% for the Congress. However, since 1967 the CPM has secured 43.4% in 1969, 29.3% in 1971, and 27.4% in 1972, while the Congress percentage has steadily increased, to an imposing 68.5% of the total in 1972! Even though there was a slight increase in the CPM percentage of the vote between 1967 and 1969, the increase was less than 5% and represented only a temporary alteration of an otherwise linear trend downward of more than 5%, hence our coding of this constituency as one of declining voter support for the CPM.

Our second example of decline is also drawn from the experience of the CPM, in this instance from the city of Durgapur (constituency # 251), a new industrial city in Burdwan District that has grown from 42,000 people in 1961 to more than 283,000 people in the 1971 census. Both the Congress and the CPM have always been strong in Durgapur, and election contests there have usually been straight fights between the two main rivals of West Bengal. However, in this rivalry the CPM has recently been bested, as is indicated by its slightly declining overall vote totals (49.6% in 1967, 51.6% in 1969, 49.1% in 1971, and 44.1% in 1972). Durgapur is a marginal case in terms of our classification, for had the CPM's vote in 1972 been half a percent higher (44.6% instead of 44.1%) we would have identified the CPM vote trend as constant across the four elections.

A third example of decline, drawn from the experience of the CPI, is Nandigram (constituency # 194), where CPI vote percentages have gone from 58.6% in 1967 to 56.4% in 1969 to 42.5% in 1971 and 46.3% in 1972. As in the case of Durgapur for the CPM, the CPI has had a basically declining vote in Nandigram, despite its continued respectable showing : thus our classification of both constituencies as exhibiting decline at high floor support levels.

Examples of Fluctuation: Constituency # 169 (Uttarpara) not only features the narrowest borderline case of fluctuation to appear in our study, it also indicates that the gods must be with the CPM in this portion of Hooghly

District.   In Uttarpara the CPM vote increased from 47.4% in 1967 to a commanding 61.2% in 1969, only to fall slightly, but for us critically, to 56.1% in 1971.   Since this latter change is 0.1% more than we allow for deviance, the CPM would have been said to have fluctuating, not growing support in Uttarpara after the 1971 election.   Continuing this pattern of "fluctuation," the CPM secured 50.007% of the vote in Uttarpara in 1972, as opposed to 49.993% for the CPI—still fluctuating support, but support that must have been pushed along by the gods.

The idea of fluctuation emerges more clearly in Manteswar constituency (# 264) in Burdwan District, one of the 34 constituencies in which the CPM charged corrupt practices by the Congress Party.   In Manteswar the CPM secured 37.4% of the vote in 1967, 60.1% in 1969, 57.1% in 1971 and only 8.7% in 1972.   These gyrations (whatever their cause) are so pronounced that it is not possible to say much about the CPM in Manteswar except that its level of support is difficult to predict.

The same might be said for a number of constituencies in which the CPI has constantly changed its electoral allies, one such example being Binpur constituency (# 219) in Midnapore District.   In Binpur the CPI garnered 26.8% of the vote in 1967 but increased its percentage to 44.6% in 1969 as a result of an electoral alliance with the CPM.   In 1971, with the CPM supporting the tribal-based Jharkhand Party in opposition to the CPI, the CPI secured only 20.1% of the vote, but this increased to 57.2% in 1972 when the CPI went into an electoral alliance with the Congress. Here we must label the CPI vote trend as fluctuation, although thus far above a floor level of 20.1%.

These categories of constancy, growth, decline, and fluctuation, combined with levels of floor support (the minimal percentage of the vote secured in any of the four elections under review), are used in Tables 5 and 6 to describe the vote trends for each Communist Party in all constituencies contested more than once since 1967.   As is indicated in Table 5, the vote for the CPM has been fluctuating in 40% (81 of 202) of the constituencies that the party has contested more than once since 1967, this being largely a reflection of the often serious dip in the CPM vote in the 1972 elections after a period of rather steady growth.   However, in three-quarters of the remaining constituencies in which the CPM has contested more than once, the party has received either constant support or overall growth, even when measured by the rather stringent criteria established for this study.   Some measure of the strength of the CPM can be gained from the fact that the CPM has suffered a decline in voter appeal in only 15% of the constituencies it has contested more than once from 1967 on, despite its disastrous showing in terms of seats won in the 1972 elections. Moreover, the CPM's vote has declined in constituencies where it has fairly high support levels, meaning that it can reasonably lose more than 5% of its vote in many of these constituencies and still remain in a competitive position relative to other parties. Its ability to compete in future contests is also enhanced by the fact that it has experienced overall growth in constituencies where its floor support is low, and where its vote has fluctuated it has done so at fairly competitive floor levels. (It should be remembered that in West Bengal's fragmented multi-party system, political parties are frequently competitive in constituencies where they can gain 25-30% of of the vote.)

TABLE 5

Vote Trends for the CPM in Constituencies Contested More Than Once (West Bengal : 1967-1972)

Levels of Floor Support	The number of constituencies in which the CPM			
	has received *constant support*	has experienced *overall* growth	has suffered a *decline* in vote	vote has been *fluctuating*
0-9% ..	—	4	1	4
10-19% ..	5	22	1	4
20-29% ..	9	23	6	22
30-39% ..	10	9	9	32
40-49% ..	6	1	13	17
50%+ ..	—	2	—	2
Total N : ..	30	61	30	81 = 202
% Total : ..	15%	30%	15%	40%
% State : ..	11%	22%	11%	29% = 72%
Average Floor Support ..	31%	23%	36%	32%

The CPI presents quite a different picture. Not only is it a much smaller party than the CPM, it has been notably less successful in building dependable support in those constituencies where it has been reasonably active. To be sure, the CPI has received constant or growing support in 40% of the constituencies it has contested more than once (see Table 6), compared with 45% for the CPM, but further examination of figures for constancy and growth reveal quite different patterns. The CPI has received constant support in only five constituencies, all at floor levels below 20%, while the CPM has received constant support in 30 constituencies, 25 of which are above the 20% floor level. Figures for constituencies in which the two parties have experienced overall growth are more comparable: the CPI has experienced growth in a third of the constituencies it has contested more than once, compared to a 30% figure for the CPM, and floor levels for both parties in these constituencies are about the same. But it should be noted that in almost all instances of CPI growth these figures merely

TABLE 6

Vote Trends for the CPI in Constituencies Contested More than Once
(West Bengal : 1967-1972)

Levels of Floor Support	The number of constituencies in which the CPI			
	has received *constant support*	has experienc-ed *overall growth*	has suffered a *decline* in vote	vote has been *fluctuating*
0-9% ..	2	2	1	1
10-19% ..	3	8	4	6
20-29% ..	—	6	6	10
30-39% ..	—	3	3	3
40-49% ..	—	1	1	2
50%+ ..	—	—	—	1
Total N : ..	5	20	15	23 = 63
% Total : ..	8%	32%	24%	37%
% State : ..	2%	7%	5%	8% = 22%
Average Floor Support ..	10%	22%	24%	25%

reflect the CPI-Congress alliance of 1972, again indicating the extent of
CPI dependence on electoral allies.   Because of this, floor support levels
for the CPI are consistently low in all categories of constituencies, and the
CPI has a far smaller percentage of constituencies in which it maintains
higher floor support levels than does the CPM.[24]

Some perspective on these figures can be gained by looking at comparable
data for the Congress Party, which tends to dominate a good many more
constituencies than both the CPI and CPM (see Table 7).   To begin with,
Congress has received constant or growing support in 108 constituencies
it has contested more than once, compared with 91 for the CPM and only 25
for the CPI.   More important is the fact that Congress has maintained much
higher floor support levels in its constituencies of constancy or growth
than has the CPM or CPI (the figures are 86 Congress constituencies maintained at floor levels above 30%, compared with only 28 CPM constituencies
of this kind and a mere four constituencies like this for the CPI).   Then
too, Congress has maintained high floor support levels in more constitu-

---

[24] Overall, floor support for the CPM exceeds 30% in half (49%) of the constituencies
which the CPM has contested more than once from 1967 to 1972, compared with less than
a quarter (22%) of the constituencies contested more than once by the CPI during this
period.

TABLE 7

Vote Trends for the Congress in Constituencies Contested More than Once
(West Bengal : 1967-1972)

Levels of Floor Support	The number of constituencies in which the Congress			
	has received *constant support*	has experienc-ed *overall growth*	has suffered a *decline* in vote	vote has been *fluctuating*
0-9% ..	—	—	2	6
10-19% ..	—	3	6	27
20-29% ..	—	19	10	38
30-39% ..	5	42	8	52
40-49% ..	3	31	2	19
50%+ ..	1	4	—	2
Total N : ..	9	99	28	144 = 280
% Total : ..	3%	35%	10%	51%
% State : ..	3%	35%	10%	51% = 99%
Average Floor Support ..	38%	36%	25%	29%

encies where its vote has fluctuated than is true either of the CPM or the CPI, and the Congress vote has declined in a smaller proportion of the constituencies it has contested (even though it has contested more consti-tuencies more often) than either the CPM or CPI. In other words, on all accounts the Congress is again the most potent party and is, therefore, the party against which the electoral opposition in West Bengal must measure its success.

THE DEPENDABILITY OF SUPPORT

It is tempting to speculate on the degree to which the two Communist parties (and the Congress) might be said to enjoy dependable support in West Bengal constituencies and to identify the levels of support which each CP can count on receiving when it contests. This, in essence, is the question of institutionalization, which for a political party means primarily the extent to which it has sunk roots in society and can secure a predictable vote in electoral competition. Insofar as a party has an identifiable level of support on which it can depend with some confidence, that party has a rational basis for calculating its prospects, both in terms of winning seats and in terms of strategic bargaining with other parties for the purpose of maximizing its potential through electoral agreements and alliances. The bargaining shrewdness shown by the CP's in the allocation of constituencies among the members of the United Front in 1969 would appear to suggest that they have considerable confidence in their ability to secure a dependably high level of support in many of the areas they have contested over the years.

On the other hand, to talk of institutionalized support in any authoritative analytical manner would be singularly ambitious given the fluid competitive environment of West Bengal and some imposing methodological constraints. The split in the Communist movement after 1962, the variegated complexion of electoral alignments involving the CP's since then, and the division in Congress itself in 1969 have conspired to produce such perpetual novelty and uncertainty in Bengali politics that prediction of anything is hazardous.

Moreover, with reference to voter appeal there is the problem of not knowing to what extent, indeed whether, the same people and groups are voting Communist in successive elections. This is no mere caveat to ward off charges of ecological fallacy. When a party is really institutionalized in a constituency, it benefits from an allegiance which may be derived from social cleavages but which assumes a largely autonomous quality. Unfortunately, we have no way of knowing how much Communist support is of this variety. There is a great deal of evidence from all over India that party fortunes still depend on prestige endorsements and "vote banks" controlled by a relatively small number of influentials. To the extent that this is so, it is a misnomer to ascribe institutionalized popular support to a party. The fluidity of Indian party politics is at least in part a reflection of the fluidity in social relations occasioned by the breakdown of traditional isolation and hierarchy. Parties seeking social roots are beneficiaries of this social ferment, but the support they acquire from it is quite unstable.

In short, several more elections—and much more research—will be required before scholars and politicians will be able to proclaim the existence of dependable support for a party with any assurance that they are referring to something real; and even then the re-delimitation of electoral units will sabotage much of the proof that would uphold such a claim.

In light of these difficulties, what we have attempted to do at this point is simply to identify the dependable vote of the CP's and the Congress over the past four elections in such a way that these data might provide insights into the degree to which a party is, or perhaps is becoming, institutionalized. In the following pages, therefore, we speak of "dependable" and "institutionalized" support, but in these instances we do so only in the broad sense conveyed above, being fully aware of the limited way in which anyone at this point can speak of dependability or institutionalization in West Bengal politics. The principal merit of such an exercise is to describe, more poignantly than we have already, the extent to which there is a significant degree of continuity in electoral performance in West Bengal despite the sweeping changes that have occurred in the state over the past decade.

There are a variety of ways in which one might try to measure the dependable or institutionalized vote of a party as exhibited in the four elections under review, but the most stringent and rigorous would be to impose the following requirements : (1) that a party have contested at least three of the four elections in the 1967-1972 period, and (2) that it have secured either a constant or growing vote. When the vote of a party has been constant over a number of elections in a rapidly changing competitive environment, we may not necessarily assume that it will remain the same over a series of succeeding elections (life is too complicated to assume any such thing); but we can infer that it would be more difficult for opposition parties to make inroads into vote totals that are maintained over long periods than it would be to affect a vote that has in the past been subject to change. In the case of growing support, we have no way of knowing how strong the party in question really is—short-term influences may affect its showing one way or another—with the result that growing support tells us less about the dependable vote of a party than does constancy. Nevertheless, a party that has growing support in a constituency certainly has some minimal level of dependable voter appeal, which we can estimate conservatively in terms of the floor vote that the party has received.

Obviously, no inferences about reliability of support would hold much weight in cases where a party's vote has been declining or where a party has contested only two or less of the past four elections in a constituency. By the same token, dependability becomes somewhat questionable when fluctuation is involved. Hence the imputation of institutionalized support is most rigorously restricted to displays of constant and increasing strength over three or four elections.

Table 8 assembles the pertinent data for such a rigorous measure. As the table points out, the CPM currently enjoys "dependable support," using this measure, in 32 (11%) of the 280 constituencies in West Bengal, while the CPI has such support in only seven constituencies (3%) and the Ruling Congress in 96 constituencies (34%). Moreover, the magnitude of the vote which the three major parties can count on in these constituencies differs considerably from party to party, with the CP's having "dependable support" at rather low levels and the Congress at comparatively high levels. One can debate the significance of the organizational split that took place in the Congress in 1969 at some length, but the fact remains that Mrs. Gandhi's Congress (R) is still the most institutionalized party in the state. The CPM may have grown at a faster pace than other parties during

TABLE 8

The Number of Constituencies Featuring Dependable Support* for the Communist Parties and Congress (West Bengal : 1967-1972)

Floor Support Levels			CPM			CPI			INC	
0-9%	..	4⎫	9% of West	2⎫	2% of West	0⎫	6% of West		
10-19%	..	12⎬	Bengal consti-	3⎬	Bengal consti-	3⎬	Bengal consti-		
20-29%	..	10⎭	tuencies	1⎭	tuencies	15⎭	tuencies		
30-39%	..	2⎫	2% of West	1		41⎫	28% of West		
40-49%	..	2⎬	Bengal consti-	0		32⎬	Bengal consti-		
50%+	..	2⎭	tuencies	0		5⎭	tuencies		
Totals	..	32		7		96			

* Dependable support is defined as a constant or growing vote in constituencies contested at least three times between 1967 and 1972.

the past decade, but one of the reasons it could do so was that it started from a very restricted base.   As Table 8 points out, Congress has dependable support in many more constituencies than does the CPM, and that support tends to be more substantial where it exists.   Whatever else these data imply, they suggest that the CPM has a long way to go before it becomes the dominant political influence in West Bengal.[25]

In some ways, however, Table 8 is misleading, if only because it tends to convey the impression that the dependable vote of the major parties of West Bengal is somehow restricted to the number of constituencies listed in the table.   A more accurate picture of the dependability of a party's vote under varying competitive situations can be gained by using our rigorous measure of "dependable support" in conjunction with data for constituencies in which the vote has fluctuated, thereby conceiving of dependability in terms of a range of constituencies that vary between definable limits.   The reason why we did not use constituencies in which parties exhibit fluctuating support in our measure of "dependable support" is that we wanted to be

[25] Table 8 distinguishes between "dependable support" at floor levels above and below 30% of the vote.   This is because it is rare for a party to win with less than 30% of the valid vote polled.   Between 1962 and 1969 no Communist candidate won in an assembly constituency with a vote under 30%.   Congress did so once, in 1967.   Given the more fragmented competitive structure of the 1971 elections in West Bengal, the CPM and Congress each won four seats and the CPI won two seats with under 30% of the vote, but the odds are very much against this happening often.   In 1972, for example, none of the three leading parties won with less than 30%, although there were several victories at or just above 30%.

as rigorous as possible in gauging dependability over time. However, by using such rigorous criteria we have consciously eliminated from our measure a large number of constituencies where there most certainly is some degree of hard-core vote for the three major parties, even if the exact magnitude of support cannot be as readily measured. If we now combine the figures in Table 8 with earlier figures for constituencies in which the vote for the major parties has been fluctuating, we should be able, in a sense, to have the best of both worlds. Our measure of "dependable support" should tell us the identifiable consistent support for each party over time in those constituencies where party support has been stable or growing, while the addition of the fluctuation figures should give us an idea of the range of constituencies in which dependability can be imputed from the record to date, albeit with reduced precision (and confidence) on the upper side of the calculation. Once again, it seems pointless to infer anything of significance with regard to constituencies contested only twice at most or in which a party's vote has been declining since 1967.

An overall picture of the dependability range of the major party vote, based on the scheme outlined above, might be described in the manner of Table 9. The most reliable vote for the CPM is in the 32 constituencies that appear in the table under the heading "dependable vote," these being constituencies where the CPM has had constant or growing support over three or four elections. At the same time, there are another 81 constituencies (enumerated as "fluctuating support") where the CPM vote has alternated by more than 5% over the course of three or four elections, but these are nevertheless places where the CPM has often done quite well. Indeed, what Table 9 points out most clearly is that the CPM vote has been more likely to fluctuate in constituencies where the party has high floor support levels and has been steady or growing in constituencies where floor support levels are rather low. What this reflects, in turn, is the ability of the CPM to maintain or expand upon many of the small electoral bases that it established at least three elections ago, and its inability to maintain or expand its totals in constituencies where it has reached peaks of voter appeal during the past decade. Its appeal in these latter constituencies is not necessarily declining, but it has varied in response to different competitive situations while in the main continuing to attract considerable support. The CPM, then, could be said to have a dependable vote of some kind in 113 constituencies (with a very regular distribution of floor levels—almost a perfect bell-shaped curve when the figures for "dependable support" and fluctuating support are added), even though it has exhibited a high degree of clearly measurable dependability in only 32 constituencies.

The "dependability range" of the CPI (between seven and 30 constituencies) is not only much lower than that for the CPM, but its floor support levels are also lower than those of the CPM in both categories of consti-

TABLE 9

Dependability Range* of The Major Party Vote in West Bengal (1967-1972)

Party	Floor Support Levels	Number of Constituencies		
		"Dependable Support" +	Fluctuating Support =	Dependability Range
CPM	0-9%	4	4	4–8
	10-19%	12	4	12–16
	20-29%	10	22	10–32
	30-39%	2	32	2–34
	40-49%	2	17	2–19
	50%+	2	2	2–4
	Totals	32	81	32–113
CPI	0-9%	2	1	2–3
	10-19%	3	6	3–9
	20-29%	1	10	1–11
	30-39%	1	3	1–4
	40-49%	0	2	0–2
	50%+	0	1	0–1
	Totals	7	23	7–30
Congress	0-9%	0	6	0–6
	10-19%	3	27	3–30
	20-29%	15	38	15–53
	30-39%	41	52	41–93
	40-49%	32	19	32–51
	50%+	5	2	5–7
	Totals	96	144	96–240

* "Dependable support" is defined as a constant or growing vote in constituencies contested at least three times between 1967 and 1972. Fluctuating support means that a party's vote has both increased and decreased by more than 5% while also varying from the base-year vote by more than 5%. The "dependability range" represents the number of constituencies at each level of floor support featuring "dependable support" at one extreme and "dependable support" plus fluctuating support at the other.

tuencies described in Table 9. This illustrates once again the dependence of the CPI on electoral allies and the extremely small base of dependable support on which the CPI can draw. A party like the CPI, which has maintained or improved its position across three or four elections in only seven constituencies, while maintaining a fluctuating vote across three or four elections in only another 23 constituencies, clearly cannot compete with the CPM or Congress as a polar force in electoral politics.

The degree to which Congress is far and away the most well-established electoral force in West Bengal emerges more clearly from these data than from any other. As can be seen from Table 9, the Congress has not only amassed constant or growing support across three or four elections in 96 constituencies, it has maintained high floor support levels in another 144 constituencies where its vote has fluctuated by more than 5% over the course of these elections. Unlike the CPM, the Congress has been able to maintain or expand its support levels in a large number of constituencies where it has always done well. Indeed, in 78 of the 96 constituencies (81%) where the Congress has "dependable support" it has maintained floor support levels of more than 30%, while the comparable figure for the CPM is only six of 32 (19%). Moreover, the Congress, like the CPM, has also maintained fairly high support levels in a large percentage of the constituencies where its vote has fluctuated by more than 5% over the course of three or four of the elections under review. The most striking aspect of the Congress profile, however, is its "dependability range" of 96 to 240 constituencies, which makes the Congress clearly the party to beat in most constituencies in the state most of the time.

IV. Party Strategies and Electoral Alliances

One of the things that emerges most clearly from the previous section is that the incidence of institutionalized or dependable support, rigorously defined, for the three major parties in West Bengal remains limited to a fairly small number of constituencies. None of these parties has established solid social bases to such an extent that it was able to secure identifiable levels of support in the bulk of West Bengal's constituencies regardless of shifting alliance patterns between 1967 and 1972. To be sure, Congress has more dependable support in more constituencies than the CPM, and the CPM has developed a more consistent base in more constituencies than the CPI; but in the majority of cases where these parties have contested at all regularly their vote fluctuated so much from one election to the next that one must necessarily characterize electoral politics in West Bengal as a process that still exhibits considerable fluidity, notwithstanding inferences of continuous underlying strength based on floor support levels in these constituencies. As in many other aspects of Indian political and social life, there is both continuity and discontinuity in electoral behaviour, while change moves along in amorphous, amoeba-like fashion despite the seemingly drastic disruptions that occasionally make headlines.

In other political systems institutionalized or dependable support can provide staying power for those who enjoy it; whatever the thrust of an election, they are not likely to be wiped out. It can also contribute continuity and predictability to the political system as a whole; the more parties having institutionalized support in more constituencies, and the greater that support is, the more structured the electoral process becomes and the easier it is to calculate what the effects of various alignments among the different competitors will be. In the case of West Bengal there is enough institutionalized support for the Congress that one would not expect it ever to be completely eliminated in an election, although some of its support could conceivably be transferred or broken up in the event of a party split. The CPM is obviously more vulnerable, but barring a major realignment of political forces, one would also expect the CPM to have a great deal of staying power in the politics of the state.

On the other hand, as our data make clear, the one thing that dependable support does not do is guarantee victory. Possessing stable support and winning seats are two ways of measuring performance, but they are largely autonomous. For example, over time the CPI has won only once in four of the seven constituencies which we have identified as giving it "dependable support," has won twice in two of the seven, and has never won in one of these constituencies. Similarly, the CPM has won only once in seven of the 32 constituencies where it has "dependable support," has won twice in only two constituencies, four times in another two constituencies, and has never won at all in 21 of these constituencies. Congress' record is somewhat better, but there is still not a strict association between dependability and victory. Congress has won nine of its 96 "dependable support" constituencies four times, 25 three times, 35 twice, 22 once, and five not at all during the four elections under review. Obviously, the prospects for victory are greater the more substantial the dependable support is, but dependable support is by no means a short-cut to victory.

The one factor that does stand out above all others as being crucial to an understanding of victory or defeat in West Bengal is the nature of party alliances in any given year, as one might expect in a fluid, competitive multi-party situation where many parties have dependable support but typically in only a few constituencies and at uncertain levels. For the major parties in the state, therefore, the "game" of electoral politics is one in which a party searches for the proper set of alliances in any given election year, in order that it can maximize the use of the dependable support it possesses, while trying to accumulate into a coalition the dependable support of others, all the time vying for the large floating vote that has not yet been consolidated by any political party. Needless to say, the game becomes even more complex than the numbers in election data can convey, if only because of the large number of factors (ideology, party financing, communal and ethnic feuds, personal ambition, and so forth) that frequently enter into alliance considerations.

Another of the advantages of looking at Bengali electoral politics, however, is that so many different kinds of alliance have been tried in the state at various times; and again, many of these have been made in elections that have a common delimitation of constituencies. In 1967 and 1971, for example, the CPI and CPM headed separate electoral coalitions that were pitted against one another, and both parties were opposed to the Congress in these years. In 1969, however, the CPI and CPM were in alliance with one another (and with 11 smaller parties), testing their combined strength against the Congress, whereas in 1972 the CPI was in alliance with the Congress against the CPM. The only combination among the major parties that has not yet been witnessed is a CPM-Congress hookup, which might be labeled unlikely were it not for the astounding ability of Bengalis to shift ground rather rapidly when circumstances dictate. At any rate, an examination of those alliances that have already been experienced provides an opportunity to observe the way in which the three major parties have interacted with one another in a number of different electoral situations in the past, and is therefore important to an understanding of the electoral performance of both CP's and the Congress in the state.

CPI-CPM Competition in 1967 and 1971

One of the conditions which has had considerable influence on Communist performance in West Bengal is the extent to which the CPI and CPM have contested against each other in the same constituencies. The Communist movement in the state experienced a series of agonizing intra-party feuds in the 1950's which were aired publicly in the early 1960's and which eventually culminated in a major party split in 1964. Ever since 1964 the two CP's have been antagonists, even though they did join the same electoral front in 1969. Party leaders have constantly attacked their counterparts of "the other party" in the press and in pamphlets; CP strategies have frequently been directed more at other Communists than at Congress; and a considerable amount of blood has been shed as a result of physical clashes between party members. The alliance effected in 1969 was more a reflection of appreciation for each other's strength than of any feeling of good will or mutual cooperation.

This state of antagonism has given rise to direct electoral competition on three occasions. In 1967 the CPI and CPM opposed one another in 38 constituencies, in 1971 they did so in 95 constituencies, and in 1972 they contested against one another 37 times. Several questions emerge from this history which our data permit us to answer. For example, where did the two parties compete in 1967, and how did each party fare under the circumstances ?   In the aftermath of the United Front of 1969, who moved in on whom in 1971 and with what effect?   How badly was each party hurt by their greatly expanded competition in 1971?   How does each party's performance in 1971 compare with what it had been previously in the same constituencies?   And finally, are the "lessons" of Communist competition in 1971 (and 1972) consistent with those of 1967?

In 1967 the CPI and CPM faced each other in 38 constituencies and worked against one another in a number of additional constituencies where their coalition partners offered candidates.   Several features of this competition stand out.   In general it would appear that the CPI and CPM fought over areas in which the united party had been active and reasonably strong.   Twenty-five of the 38 constituencies are located in the Calcutta-Durgapur industrial grid, another seven are located in and along the eastern strip of 24-Parganas, and the remaining six are in northern Bengal.   The redelimitation of 1966 precludes direct comparisons with the 1962 elections, but on the basis of more impressionistically derived equivalences it would appear that the united CPI had contested 32 of these constituencies in 1962, securing a rather high average vote of 47% in them.   Moreover, while the united party had won less than 17% of the seats in the state legislative assembly in 1962, it had won almost half (17) of the seats where the CPI and CPM confronted one another in 1967.   Direct competition between the two CP's, therefore, was primarily the result of each party's attempts to retain previous Communist strongholds.

The way things turned out in 1967 confirmed the regional nature of the Communist split in West Bengal.   Just as the split was largely segmental, with the CPM inheriting the West Bengal heartland and the CPI inheriting the south-eastern perimeter, so too in the constituencies in which they contested against each other one party tended to do very much better than the other, where being consistent with the regional division.   Since most of the constituencies in question fall within the industrial conurbation, the CPM came out well ahead in the competition.   The CPM secured more votes than the CPI in 28 of the 38 constituencies where the two parties contested and won nine seats, as opposed to five for the CPI.[26]

On the other hand, granting that the CPM emerged as the larger and stronger party in the wake of the Communist split, there is reason to believe that the CPI was more effective in undercutting the CPM in its areas of post-split dominance than was the CPM in CPI areas, even though both parties demonstrated survival ability in the face of a strong challenge from the other.   The CPI won five of the ten constituencies in which it outpolled the CPM despite the division in the Communist vote.   Four of these wins

---

[26] Two of the CPI's victories when opposed by the CPM were in Midnapore, two in eastern 24-Parganas, and one in Calcutta.

came in areas that the united party had lost in 1962. By contrast, the CPM won only nine of the 28 constituencies in which it prevailed over the CPI, a considerable decline from the 15 wins of the united party in these areas five years before. No doubt some of variation in performance may be attributed to the changes in constituency boundaries which took place between the Third and Fourth General Elections. Even so, the comparison of 1967 results with those for 1962 does suggest that the CPI may be in a better position to hurt the CPM when the two parties run against each other than the CPM is in a position to hurt the CPI. On the basis of these data one might conclude that CPI strength is less dependent on what the CPM does than the reverse.

The election in 1971 provides an excellent test of this inference as well as an enlarged arena for examining what happens when Communists compete against each other. The CPI and CPM in 1971 came into direct conflict in 95 constituencies, more than a third of the total for the state as a whole and well in excess of the 38 they fought in the first time. Moreover, the great majority of these constituencies had been contested by one party or the other in 1969. ꞏIt is therefore possible to examine what happened when tactical cooperation was replaced by open electoral challenge.

One way of looking at the impact that CPI-CPM competition had on each party in 1971 is to distinguish between constituencies contested by the CPI two years earlier under the aegis of the United Front and those contested by the CPM. (In most instances these were constituencies which the party in question had contested in 1967 as well and if challenged by its Communist rival had done notably better, obliging the rival to yield in 1969.) Based on which CP was there in 1969, it is possible to think of constituencies in which the CPI moved in on the CPM in 1971 and others in which the CPM intruded on the CPI. Both parties intruded quite often. The CPI entered CPM constituencies on 37 occasions, and in 30 constituencies the CPM challenged the established presence of the CPI.[27]

An important aspect of this mutual vendetta is that most of these constituencies had been won by the CP present there in 1969. The CPI had been victorious in 24 of the 30 constituencies now being entered by the CPM, and the CPM had won a spectacular 34 of the 37 constituencies now being entered by the CPI. As we shall see, the CP's had helped each other do as well as each did quite often in 1969 through transferred support. Now, in 1971, the idea was to achieve the opposite effect. Hostility between the two parties had reached a high point; and it is clear that each party sought to undermine the other, particularly in the case of the

---

[27] In addition, the CPI and CPM confronted one another in 28 constituencies in which neither party had sponsored candidates in 1969. See note 33 below.

CPI's wanting to chasten the CPM. A central objective of the CPI in the 1971 elections was to deny the CPM votes essential to winning the number of seats necessary to gain access to the state Government once again.

Each intruding party did modestly well in 1971, regaining its former vote in those constituencies it had contested in 1967 all but once (in fact, often improving on its earlier performance) and in most instances securing a respectable vote in constituencies entered for the first time.[28]   The CPM managed to win six seats from the CPI, while the CPI won two seats from the CPM.[29]   Each party succeeded in siphoning votes away from the other, as intended, in the great majority of cases, producing additional losses in the process. (These were seats picked up by third parties, usually Mrs. Gandhi's Congress.) All in all, both CP's could view their efforts to enter the other's domain and inflict damage with a measure of satisfaction.

But if each party was hurt by the competition, the vital statistics make it clear that the CPI was hurt a great deal more than the CPM, belying the inferences drawn from their competition in 1967. This is apparent if we examine each party's record in those constituencies where it had been contesting regularly prior to 1971. The following direct comparisons and Table 10 summarize the pertinent data:

: The CPI vote dropped from 1969 to 1971 in all 30 constituencies in which the CPM intruded, usually by a considerable amount (average change $= -27\%$). The CPM held or increased its vote in 14 of the 37 constituencies entered by the CPI. The average change in the CPM vote was -9% overall.[30]

: In 20 of 25 constituencies the CPI's vote was appreciably lower in 1971 than it had been in 1967. The CPM vote was lower in only six of 37 constituencies. The average change in the CPI's vote was -16% between the two years, as opposed to an average change of $+8\%$ for the CPM. (See Table 10 for the mean percent vote attained by each party in these constituencies.)

---

[28] The CPM was especially successful in these new constituencies, securing an average vote of 27% (N=17) and forfeiting only three deposits. The average vote for the CPI under similar circumstances was 16% (N=22), with deposits lost 15 times. Although less impressive than the CPM's record, the CPI's level of support in these constituencies was better than most newcomers are normally able to acquire given the reasonably well institutionalized vote in West Bengal.

[29] Five of these six wins for the CPM occurred in constituencies which the party had not contested before.

[30] As in our earlier discussion, we do not consider a vote to have declined unless it is more than 5% lower than previously. For example, in Tollygunge constituency of Calcutta the CPM vote was 63% in 1969 and 59% in 1971. We consider Tollygunge to be a case in which the CPM held its vote. We might add that in no instance can a decline in support for the CPI or CPM in 1971 be traced to the return of another former ally in these constituencies.

: Across the three elections (1967, 1969, and 1971) the CPM sustained its strength well enough in more than a third of the constituencies in which it was challenged by the CPI to have "dependable support" in them according to our criteria, with 12 of the 14 constituencies in question actually showing overall growth at the time. The CPI failed to demonstrate that it had "dependable support" in any of its constituencies when challenged by the CPM.

: Because of their competition against each other, both parties lost seats in 1971 that they had won in 1969; but the CPI was much more seriously affected by the competition than the CPM in this regard. The CPI lost 17 of the 24 seats in which it had been victorious two years before, while the CPM was defeated in only seven of the 34 it had won. Moreover, the CPM won in two constituencies for the first time despite competition from the CPI.

: When faced with CPM opposition in 1971, the CPI won fewer seats (7) than it had attained in the same constituencies in 1967 (11). By contrast, in constituencies entered by the CPI in 1971 the CPM emerged with almost twice as many victories as in 1967 (29 and 15 respectively).

TABLE 10

Communist Competition: Average Percent Vote for the CPI and CPM from 1967 to 1971 When One Party Intruded on the Other in 1971[a]

			CPM Intruded on the CPI[b]			CPI Intruded on the CPM[c]		
			1967	1969	1971	1967	1969	1971
CPI	..	..	40%	53%	26%	15%	—	19%
CPM	..	..	19%	—	27%	40%	57%	48%

[a] One party is said to have intruded on the other when it entered a constituency in 1971 which the other had contested in 1969 and contested again in 1971.

[b] N=30 constituencies for 1969 and 1971. The CPI contested 25 of these constituencies in 1967 and the CPM contested 13. The 1967 figures are based on these numbers.

[c] N=37 constituencies for the CPM all three years and for the CPI in 1971. In 1967 the CPI contested 15 of these constituencies.

In short, the CPI took a fearful beating at the hands of the CPM in 1971 both in terms of votes taken from its candidates and seats lost. The CPI's predicament would seem to be well summarized in the case of Ashokenagar constituency (# 81) in 24-Parganas. In 1967 both the CPI and the CPM put up candidates in Ashokenagar, the CPI coming out the stronger and winning the seat narrowly with 34% of the vote compared to Congress' 32% and the CPM's 29%. With CPM assistance in 1969 the same CPI candidate, Sadhan Kumar Sen, amassed 56% of the vote, soundly defeating his Congress opponent. However, in 1971 the CPM reentered the constituency, acquiring 43% of the vote, enough to win, while dropping Sadhan Kumar Sen of the CPI to third place, behind Congress (R), with only 22% of the vote.[31] Although the CPM did not usually win in constituencies of this kind, Ashokenagar illustrates what the data show to be true generally in 1971, namely the CPI's vulnerability in the face of CPM opposition. The CPM actually secured a greater vote than the CPI in 17 of the 30 constituencies like Ashokenagar in 1971, and this is reflected in the slightly larger average vote for the CPM shown in the table. The CPM also won almost as many seats as the CPI in these constituencies (six and seven respectively).

In comparison, the CPM fared very much better when challenged by the CPI. As Table 10 indicates, the CPM remained very strong in these 37 constituencies, notwithstanding CPI efforts to erode its position. The constituency of Hirapur ($\#$ 244) in Burdwan District is fairly representative. Both the CPM and CPI contested the Hirapur seat in 1967, with the CPM doing very much better (37% of the vote to the CPI's 17%) yet losing narrowly to Congress (38%). The CPM remained in Hirapur in 1969 as the United Front's representative, and with the help of the CPI it managed to win the seat with a solid 58% of the vote in a straight fight against Congress. In 1971 the CPI returned to the constituency, sponsoring a candidate of its own against the CPM incumbent. The CPI managed to get its 1967 vote back (17%) and in the process made a modest dent in the CPM's support compared with what it had been two years before. Yet the CPM still secured 45% of the vote, down 13% from 1969 but a decided improvement over 1967 (when the CPM had 37% of the vote) and enough to win the Hirapur seat once again.

The case of Hirapur illustrates several points of generic relevance. The CPI did credibly well in these constituencies, at least on the basis of its performance in 1967; and it did cost the CPM votes. Nevertheless, the CPM remained strong enough to win in most instances, in part because it would seem to have held on to some of the support transferred to it in 1969 or else to have succeeded in acquiring new support apart from Front contributions. Either way the CPM's position had become distinctly more solid that it was in 1967. Barring spectacular breakthroughs for the CPI, which were rare, the CPM was not seriously affected by the CPI's entry or return to the constituencies which it (the CPM) had contested in 1969. Whereas the CPM had a distinctly undermining effect on the CPI in the

---

[31] The decline in the CPI's fortunes cannot be attributed to the performance of Congress (R) in Ashokenagar. The Congress (R) candidate secured 32% of the vote in 1971, the same as Congress had received in 1969 and 1967.

reverse circumstances, it was relatively immune to CPI opposition in 1971. Indeed, consideration of all these constituencies together reveals that while the CPI suffered a net loss of 15 seats, the CPM actually made a gain of one.[32]

What emerges from this analysis is a picture of Communist competition which should be sobering to those prone to see in the Communist split or in CPI-CPM competition a death knell to Communist fortunes in West Bengal. Not only is the CPM infinitely stronger today than the united party was at the peak of its strength in 1962, the CPM has shown that it is capable of withstanding opposition from the CPI remarkably well while at the same time punishing the CPI severely in its constituencies (and outmuscling the CPI in new constituencies),[33] at least when the CPI is not in alliance with Congress. There is no way of knowing precisely how much better the CPM would have done in the absence of a challenge from the CPI, but the comparison of CPM performance in 1969 and 1971 reveals that the CPI's intrusions were not terribly consequential. Whereas the CPI owed much of the dramatic downturn in its fortunes in 1971 to competition from the CPM,[34] the CPM came out of these contests surprisingly unaffected by opposition from the CPI. It lost a modest share of votes but very few seats, and these were more than counterbalanced by new victories. The CPI, on the other hand, lost both votes and seats in profusion. The beneficiary of CPM support in 1969, the CPI plummeted in the face of CPM opposition in 1971.

THE CONTRIBUTION OF THE UNITED FRONT TO COMMUNIST SUCCESSES IN 1969

A dramatically different competitive configuration existed in 1969, when the CPI and CPM coordinated their strategies with one another and with almost every other party in the state to produce a truly United Front

---

[32] The CPI lost 17 seats it had won in 1969 and picked up two from the CPM. The CPM lost seven seats it had won previously, but won eight new seats (six from the CPI and two in spite of CPI opposition). None of the seats lost by the CPM had been won in 1967, whereas seven of the CPI's losses occurred in constituencies which the CPI had won twice before.

[33] Of the 28 constituencies featuring CPI-CPM competition in 1971 which neither party had contested in 1969, the CPM's vote exceeded the CPI's in all but four constituencies and averaged out at twice the overall level of support (29% of the vote for the CPM, 15% for the CPI). The CPM won six of these 28 constituencies and provided the principal opposition in 15 others. The CPI won but once and finished second only three times. On the other hand, the CPI forfeited 18 deposits compared with only five deposits lost by CPM candidates..

[34] All but three of the CPI's net losses in 1971 (from 30 seats to 13) occurred in the context of competition from the CPM.

against Congress.   So thorough were the pre-election negotiations among the Front parties that in no constituency did they end up contesting against each other.[35]   Every constituency in which the Front ran featured a single Front candidate, usually from the member party which had previously demonstrated the greatest strength in that particular location.

There are two ways in which the Communist parties might have benefited from the United Front of 1969.   First, coalition allies which had contested against the CPI or CPM in 1967 might drop out of certain constituencies with the intent of transferring their support to the remaining CP.   Second, in the allocation of seats for each member of the UF to contest in 1969, the CP's might be given constituencies in which they had not been present in 1967.   While the Communists could certainly move into such constituencies even without the UF, doing so within the framework of the broad alliance would offer at least the prospect of securing the support which had gone to their new allies two years before.

Both patterns were at work in 1969.   The CPI was given exclusive competitive position in 12 constituencies in which one ally or another had also contested in 1967 (ten were yielded by the CPM and two by the SSP).   In addition, the CPI moved into five constituencies which in 1967 had been contested by the CPM, Bangla Congress, and—in one instance— by a strong independent.   The CPM did even better, carrying the Front banner in 55 constituencies, all but two of which had featured competition against other Front members in 1967.[36]   In return, the CPI withdrew from 31 constituencies (most of which went to the CPM), and the CPM yielded 38 (13 in all to the CPI, 10 to the Forward Bloc, eight to the Bangla Congress, with the rest dispersed among lesser parties and an independent).

In other words, the United Front in 1969 was a major exercise in political juggling, perhaps the most adventuresome undertaking of its kind in all of India since independence in terms of both the number of parties involved and the number of constituencies affected (99, or 35% of the state's 280 constituencies).

Even so, it is important for perspective to note that in a considerable number of constituencies contested by the CP's in 1969 (19 of 36 for the

---

[35] An excellent discussion of the detailed strategic planning that parties in India engage in when building electoral coalitions appears in Bruce Bueno de Mesquita, "A Model of Coalition Behavior: The Case of India (1967-1971)," Ph. D. dissertation, University of Michigan, 1971.

[36] Twenty-five of these constituencies were yielded to the CPM by the CPI.   Sixteen came from the Bangla Congress, along with one other in which both the CPI and the Bangla Congress had been present; ten were contributed by the Forward Bloc and one by the SSP (the only one from a party aligned with the CPM in 1967), while two new constituencies were taken over from the Bangla Congress in one instance and from an independent in the other.

CPI and 42 of 97 for the CPM) the Front was not a factor at all. This is relevant insofar as any explanation of Communist successes which stresses the United Front is concerned, especially as most of these constituencies were won by the CP's in 1969. The CPI was on its own 53% of the time and the CPM 43%. Moreover, even when the Front did play a role, the CP's had won quite a few constituencies in 1967 anyway despite the divisions among the non-Congress parties. The CPI had won five of the 12 constituencies also contested by another UF member, and the CPM had won 22 of the 53 in which it had faced competition from a new ally. In short, based on projections from 1967 the CPI might have anticipated securing 16 seats in the 1969 poll even without Front help (the number it actually did win in 1967), and the CPM might have felt that it could reproduce 38 of its victories.

Inherited strength notwithstanding, the Front provided both CP's with the opportunity to win a number of seats which had either eluded them in 1967 or for which they had not even put up candidates. The mechanism of the new successes would be transfers of support from allies relinquishing the constituencies in favour of the CP's under the UF arrangements. Each CP entered a constituency which had been won by a UF partner in 1967 (the Bangla Congress both times). If they could get the better part of the Bangla Congress vote in these two constituencies, each CP would have another win.[37]

TABLE 11

Protected Communist Victories in West Bengal, 1969, Based on Past Performance and Anticipated Strength Resulting from Vote Transfers

	CPI	CPM
Seats won in 1967		
Front allies not there	11	16
Front allies there	5	22
Front ally won in 1967	1	1
Potential victories based on transferred support ..	7	19
Total ..	24 of 36 seats contested	58 of 97 seats contested
% of seats contested	67%	60%
% of seats in state	9%	21%

[37] The Bangla Congress had won both constituencies (Karimpur, in Nadia District, and Hasnabad, in 24-Parganas) by substantial margins. As things turned out, the CPI did receive most of the Bangla vote or at least enough of it plus a smaller CPM vote to win in Hasnabad. In Karimpur, however, the CPM received less than half of the Bangla vote and lost very narrowly (by 0.1%) to Congress, which clearly attracted some of that support itself.

More important were the constituencies in which the combined Front-CP vote in 1967 would be enough to produce victory if repeated and transferred. Going into the 1969 contest, the CPI could have anticipated seven additional victories based solely on transferred help while the CPM could look forward to 19 new seats if it held its own support and received the votes intended for it by its new friends in the coalition. In 13 constituencies (12 pertaining to the CPM) a full transfer would not be enough to win unless Congress support declined or the CP's marshaled votes from other sources. Excluding these, Table 11 summarizes the plausible projections which each Communist party might have made in preparing for the 1969 elections in West Bengal on the basis of its own past performance and the known strength of its allies two years earlier.

If all went well, the CPI could win two-thirds of the seats it contested (24 of 36) and the CPM could win 58 of its 97, or three-fifths. Both performances would be better than Communists had ever done before in the state; and seats won by other means—by no stretch of the imagination an impossibility—would be an added bonus. Moreover, given the existing seats of other Front members and the levels of support to be transferred from the CP's to their allies and among the other coalition members, there was a very real prospect of winning enough seats to keep Congress from power and of forming a second UF Government in which the CP's would have a central position.

Both Communist parties in fact did better than these projective calculations suggest, and at first glance at least it would seem that the United Front was even more successful than anticipated. The number of seats won by Congress declined from 127 to a shockingly low 55, while the Front parties either held their own or won many more seats than they ever had before. Although there were many more parties on the West Bengal ballots in 1969 than in 1967, in fact the 1969 elections were much more bipolar; and it can reasonably be assumed that Congress losses were a function of United Front gains. Indeed, what is so intriguing about the 1969 poll is how similar the percentage of the vote for different key parties at the state level was to the 1967 figures and yet how different the results.[38]

The importance of the Front is also conveyed by the added support secured by the CPI and CPM, particularly in comparison with the change in the Congress vote in the same constituencies. These data are shown in Table 12. In the aggregate, the vote intended for the CP's would seem to have gone to them. Whereas the Communist share of the vote increased by an average of 7% or 8% when the Front was not in a position to lend

---

[38] For example, Congress polled 41.1% of the vote in 1967 and 41.3% in 1969. Figures for other leading parties are as follows: CPM—18.1% and 20.0%; CPI—6·5% and 7.0%; Bangla Congress—10.2% and 8.2%; Forward Bloc—4.4% and 5.0%.

TABLE 12

Changes in the Communist and Congress Vote Related to the "Available" Vote of Departing Front Parties (West Bengal): 1967-1969[a]

	Available Front Vote[b]	CP Vote Change	Congress Vote Change
CPI Contested in 1969			
Front ally present in 1967 :			
CPM (N=10)	17%	+15%	+2%
SSP (N=2)	9%	+23%	−4%
No Front ally present (N=19) ..	—	+ 7%	+2%
CPM Contested in 1969			
Front ally present in 1967 :			
CPI (N=25)	14%	+18%	−1%
Other (N=27)	15%	+14%	−6%
CPI & Other (N=1) ..	22%	+21%	+4%
No Front ally present (N=42) ..	—	+ 8%	−3%

[a] This table does not include the seven constituencies in which the CP contesting in 1969 was absent in 1967.

[b] The "available Front vote" is the level of support which the yielding Front candidates received in 1967.

support, it jumped notably higher when the Front was a factor. Moreover, there is a marked similarity in the vote available to the CP's and the magnitude of increase in CP support. The one obvious variation concerns only two constituencies, where the CPI vote increased by more than the SSP could have provided. But the overall pattern is strongly suggestive of successful transfers of support to the CP's from their allies, including each other. Such an interpretation is made all the more credible by the fact that changes in the Congress vote were very much lower and that these changes do not relate at all meaningfully to the available UF vote. It would appear that Congress received very little of this vote and that, as intended, the CP's got most or all of it.

Aggregate statistics, of course, may conceal a great amount of variation among constituencies and obfuscate different relationships within constituencies. For these reasons we have made an attempt to establish the actual fact and magnitude of transferred support in each constituency contested by a UF partner in 1967 but yielded to one CP or the other under the Front arrangements in 1969. This is necessarily a crude exercise, yet an unavoidable one if the contribution of the Front to Communist successes in 1969 is to be assessed with modest rigor.

The obvious problem with such an undertaking is that it is impossible to pinpoint the existence and size of a transfer. If the CP vote increased in 1969 over what it had been in 1967, we do not know for sure whether that increase was occasioned by the added support made available by a departing ally, even if the figures are similar; whether some, much, or all of it came from other sources; or whether it simply reflects growing Communist strength based on their own efforts. We were therefore obliged to make a few assumptions which may or may not be valid in each case.

First, when the CP's contested both years we had to assume that their 1967 percentage of the vote was replicated in 1969 and that any support left over might be the product of a transfer. If the Communist vote declined in 1969, we could not credit what support was received to the assistance of an ally, although the assistance may have been real and without it the Communist vote would have declined even further. When the CP's entered constituencies in 1969 which they did not contest in 1967, the only basis for asserting that a transfer took place was if the party in question won at least a requisite portion of what its ally or allies had polled in 1967.

For a transfer to be acknowledged we required two conditions: (1) that at least one UF partner was active in the constituency in 1967 with its own candidate on the ballot, and (2) that the Communist party running in 1969 have a vote increase over 1967 which is greater than half the percentage vote which the departing UF partner(s) received. In the seven constituencies of new CP entries in 1969 we accepted as successful transfers only those instances in which the Communist vote was more than half of the percentage vote attained by the UF ally(ies) present in 1967. In other words, we do not (because we cannot) identify a vote transfer if the party presumably contributing its support did not compete in the constituency in 1967. Nor do we accept as a transfer any apparent increment of support for the CP's even when an ally was present and had an identifiable magnitude of support which it might have attempted to bestow upon the CP's. In order to be modestly stringent we have stipulated that if the CP in question did not appear to receive more than half of the available Front vote in a constituency—given the assumptions noted above—a transfer would not be recognized. In such circumstances we would consider the available vote to have been dissipated among the remaining candidates or at least not to have assisted the CP in the way intended by the Front coalition.

It might be helpful to mention a few examples of successful transfer by way of illustration. The scheduled caste constituency of Ukhra in Burdwan District seems to have featured a perfect transfer of support from the Bangla Congress to the CPM, enabling the CPM to win the Ukhra seat in 1969 in a straight fight against Congress despite the fact that Congress did just as well as it had in 1967, when it won the seat. The same candidates ran for the CPM and Congress both years, and voter turnout was at the same basic level. Victory for the CPM is clearly attributable to votes bequeathed by its Bangla Congress ally.

TABLE 13

Transferred Support in Ukhra Constituency (SC): # 250

1967		1969	
Party by Place of Finish	% Vote	Party by Place of Finish	% Vote
1. Congress	47	1. CPM	54
2. CPM	40	2. Congress	46
3. Bangla Congress ..	13		

In the constituency of Jalpaiguri (Jalpaiguri District) the CPI received immense support from the CPM to prevail over Congress, which had won handsomely in 1967 and had actually improved its own vote in 1969. It would appear that the CPM did not effect a complete transfer of its support to the CPI, yet because the CPI vote increased by more than half of the available CPM strength (80% in this case) we consider a successful transfer to have been achieved in Jalpaiguri benefiting the CPI.

TABLE 14

Transferred Support in Jalpaiguri Constituency: # 18

1967		1969	
Party by Place of Finish	% Vote	Party by Place of Finish	% Vote
1. Congress	42	1. CPI	51
2. CPI	29	2. Congress	46
3. CPM	27	3. Jana Sangh	2
4. Independent	2	4. Independent	1

Finally, the constituency of Chandrakona in Midnapore District illustrates an instance in which a CP's vote increased from 1967 to 1969 by a larger amount than the available support from an ally can account for. While the difference is not great, it would appear that the CPM in Chandrakona received not only the Bangla Congress vote but also some support from the independent who dropped the constituency in 1969. In addition, voter participation was notably higher in the mid-term poll, and this may have helped the CPM as well. In any event, it is clear that a transfer took place.

TABLE 15

Transferred Support in Chandrakona Constituency: # 185

1967		1969	
Party by Place of Finish	% Vote	Party by Place of Finish	% Vote
1. Congress	39	1. CPM	57
2. CPM	30	2. Congress	43
3. Bangla Congress ..	23		
4. Independent	8		

We might also note two cases in which transfers might have occurred but, by our standards, did not. In the urban constituency of Kharagpur in Midnapore District the CPI appeared to be in an excellent position, with CPM assistance, to hold on to a seat it had won rather narrowly in 1967. As things turned out, however, the CPI not only failed to amass the small if potentially critical CPM vote, it actually lost support of its own. To the extent that any transfer was effected in Kharagpur, Congress

TABLE 16

The Failure of Transfer in Kharagpur Constituency: # 211

1967		1969	
Party by Place of Finish	% Vote	Party by Place of Finish	% Vote
1. CPI	49	1. Congress	55
2. Congress	44	2. CPI	44
3. CPM	7	3. Jana Sangh	.5
		4. National Democratic Front	.5
		5. Independent	.2

was the beneficiary. In Karimpur constituency in Nadia District the CPM replaced the Bangla Congress, which had achieved a landslide victory in 1967. This move backfired for the Front. Had the CPM been able to command even half of the Bangla vote it would have won despite a much improved performance by Congress. The failure of the intended transfer enabled Congress to squeak by in the closest election in the state that year.

TABLE 17

The Failure of Transfer in Karimpur Constituency: # 64

1967			1969			
Party by Place of Finish		% Vote	Party by Place of Finish			% Vote
1. Bangla Congress	..	69	1. Congress	..	..	33.7
2. Congress	.. ..	22	2. CPM	..	..	33.6
3. Independent	.. ..	9	3. Independent	..	..	30
			4. Proutist Bloc		..	3

When one looks at the overall picture, the incidence of transfer is most impressive for both Communist parties. Given our criteria, the CPI can be said to have received the requisite level of support from its UF allies in 14 of the 17 constituencies where transfers were a possibility. This figure includes the two cases where the SSP was the presumed donor, seven of the ten constituencies yielded by the CPM after competing against the CPI in 1967, and all five of the constituencies entered by the CPI as the Front representative in 1969.[39]

For its part the CPM can be said to have received transfers 50 out of 55 times: in 24 of 25 constituencies yielded by the CPI, 14 of 16 yielded by the Bangla Congress, nine of ten ceded by the Forward Bloc, the one yielded by the SSP, and one of the two constituencies entered in 1969. The pervasiveness of transfers for both parties and from all donors precludes discrimination based on which UF partners were most reliable sources of support. All were quite dependable.[40] Moreover, the magnitude of the transfers was considerable, the mean size of those going to the CPI being 17% and of those going to the CPM being 14%.[41]

---

[39]In the three constituencies in which transfers did not take place, the CPI vote itself declined. Besides Kharagpur, these constituencies are Basirhat (24-Parganas) and Moyna (Midnapore), both of which the CPI won anyway.

[40]Another way of putting this is that the CP's were sufficiently attractive to the voters of other parties that transfers were quite easy to effect. In three of the five cases when no transferral of support could be detected for the CPM, the CPM vote itself declined. One other case was that of Karimpur constituency, considered above. The final case was a very near miss.

[41]Only constituencies in which each CP contested both years are included in these tabulations. When the increase in each party's support exceeded the available Front support, we accepted the available Front vote as the amount of transfer. When each party's increase was less than the available vote, the increase itself is the amount of transfer.

These data on the incidence and magnitude of transferred support would seem to sustain the hypothesis that the Communists, especially the CPM, did so well in West Bengal in the 1969 mid-term poll precisely because they were central members and beneficiaries of the elaborate United Front alliance. Although the Front was not a factor in quite a number of constituencies contested by the CP's in 1969 (19 for the CPI and 42 for the CPM) and although no transfers could be detected in a few additional cases even when they were possible, the general impression conveyed by the material we have been considering is that the Front helped the Communists often and consequentially.

A look at the actual election results corroborates this argument, in the main, but at the same time introduces a note of caution, lest the contribution of the United Front be over-interpreted. The Front's contribution may be seen in the fact that in seven of the nine constituencies in which the CPI received UF transfers, it won in 1969 whereas it had previously lost. The CPI also won three of the five new constituencies it contested in 1969 thanks to the UF arrangements. These ten victories account for all but four of the additional seats won by the CPI in 1969 as against 1967. Similarly, the CPM appears to have benefited considerably from the support transferred by its allies. Twenty-six constituencies featuring transfers were won by the CPM in 1969 following losses in 1967. Considering that the CPM won 37 more seats in 1969 than it had two years earlier, much of its gains would seem to reflect Front assistance.[42]

On the other hand, there are nagging little suggestions in the data which question the prominence of the Front. The CPM also won 17 seats it had lost in 1967 even though no allies were in a position to transfer support; the CPI won five new seats under the same circumstance. The CPM repeated a previous win 16 times when the Front was not a factor; the CPI did so 11 times. Even when the Front was relevant each party won twice without benefit of a transfer. Moreover, when transfers were recorded, the CPM won in 19 constituencies that it had won without the Front in 1967, indicating that the transfers were not the basis for this considerable number of victories. (The CPI won only two constituencies in which the contribution of transferred support may be questioned in this fashion.)

Finally, both parties gained votes in 1969 above and beyond what they seem to have garnered from transfers. CPI vote increases exceeded the available UF support in six of the nine constituencies the CPI contested twice. Eliminating the transfers, the mean increase in CPI support from

---

[42]The CPM won neither of the constituencies it entered for the first time in 1969, although it lost both by less than a percentage point, once because the intended transfer failed and once because the transfer plus other support was not enough.

these constituencies is a solid 11%. The CPI vote also surpassed the UF vote in four of the five new constituencies, once by more than 40%. The CPM vote increased by more than the available transfers in 33 of 49 constituencies, with a mean of 6% after the transfers are taken into account. The CPM also exceeded the UF vote in one of its two new constituencies by 11%.

In other words, as many as 18 victories for the CPI and 35 for the CPM had nothing to do with transferred support, while the role of the Front is questionable in 21 other constituencies in which transfers can be identified, if only because the CP's had previously won them all without UF support. Elsewhere it is possible that the CP's achieved new victories

TABLE 18

The Importance of Transferred Support to Communist Victories in 1969

The Instrumental Value of a Transfer	Constituencies in which the CPI Received Transferred Support		
	New Victories	Also Won in 1967	Total: CPI Wins (1969)
	(N)	(N)	(N)
Vital	4	2 ..	6
Helpful	4	1 ..	5
Inconsequential	1	— ..	1
Totals ..	9	3 ..	12

The Instrumental Value of a Transfer	Constituencies in which the CPM Received Transferred Support		
	New Victories	Also Won in 1967	Total: CPM Wins (1969)
	(N)	(N)	(N)
Vital	12	4 ..	16
Helpful	13	15 ..	28
Inconsequential	1	— ..	1
Totals ..	26	19 ..	45

Note: A "vital" transfer is one which made the difference between victory and defeat. A "helpful" transfer was not essential to victory but was nevertheless large enough to account for more than a fifth of the gain in the CP vote in 1969. An "inconsequential" transfer amounted to less than a fifth of the growth in CP support.

as much from their own stronger appeal to the electorate as from transfers. When all is said and done, one wonders whether the link between United Front support and Communist successes in 1969 is not more coincidence than causality.

Given this lingering uncertainty about the significance of transfers, we have probed further into our data, asking how instrumental transferred support to the CP's in fact was.

Table 18 shows constituencies won by each CP in 1969 when a transfer can be identified. The distribution is arranged in terms of how critical transfers were to the victories achieved. A "vital" transfer is one that marked the difference between victory and defeat. Had the CP in question not received the transfer it would have lost. In these cases we can assert that the transfer was indispensable to a Communist win. A "helpful" transfer is one which was not essential to victory in that the CP would have won without it but which was nevertheless large enough to account for much of the gain in the CP vote in 1969. An "inconsequential" transfer, by contrast, not only failed to affect the outcome, it failed to represent a significant part of the overall increase in Communist strength. Operationally we have identified as inconsequential transfers those which amount to less than a fifth of the growth in CP support since 1967. This is an arbitrary cut-off point, but we believe it is intuitively reasonable.[43]

The findings reported in Table 18 may come as a surprise to those who would attribute the notable successes of the CPM and CPI in 1969 primarily to the added support provided by their United Front allies. Even though most of the seats won with the help of transferred support had been lost in 1967, the transfers themselves account for less than half of the new victories attained by each CP with discernible coalition support. That is to say, the CP's would have won a majority of these constituencies even without the UF support they received.[44]

---

[43] Logically it is possible for a transfer to be both essential to victory yet insignificant in terms of the overall growth of a party's support. With this apparent inconsistency in mind we checked each constituency in which a vital transfer was identified benefiting one CP or the other. We can assure the reader that insofar as one can establish the magnitude of transfers to begin with, a vital transfer was the dominant source of increased party support in each case.

[44] The validity of this exercise to establish the instrumental value of a transfer is enhanced in the case of the CPM by reference to the 1971 election results in these same constituencies. In 1971 the CPM again won 26 of the 29 constituencies in which transferred support was at best "helpful." Defeats were more common when the transferred support had been "vital." (The CPM lost seven of 16 seats in this category.) This is as we would have predicted. The CPM continued to win when its own share of the vote was sufficient, but it was prone to lose in constituencies where vote transfers had made the difference between victory and defeat two years before. That the CPM won a majority of the constituencies in which its victories in 1969 had been based on "vital" transfers is due primarily to the fact

To be sure, only on two occasions were identifiable transfers so dwarfed by the overall gains in Communist votes as to be inconsequential to improved performance. Moreover, in several instances (six in all) transfers actually saved a CP from losing seats previously won. We might also note that had the United Front not existed and had the CPM lost the 16 seats it won as a result of the Front, the CPM would not have emerged as the largest party in the West Bengal legislative assembly in 1969.[45]

Yet it is clear that the United Front of 1969 was not nearly as important to the success of the Communist parties as is generally supposed. Votes transferred to the CPI were the difference between victory and defeat in only six constituencies, half the number of those won in which transfers were a factor. Vital transfers benefiting the CPM were more numerous but represent only a third of the cases in which transfers are nominally associated with CPM victories. Both Communist parties owed a fifth, but no more than a fifth, of their victories in 1969 to the grand alliance against Congress.[46]

THE CPI-CONGRESS ALLIANCE IN 1972

If the United Front alliance of 1969 can be described as being of limited (but important) value to the CP's, the CPI-Congress alliance of 1972 was much more valuable to the CPI. In 1972 the CPI contested 41 constituencies, none of which were contested by the Congress Party, and in the vast majority of these constituencies both the Congress and CPI organizations were working for the CPI candidate. As one might expect, the CPM also contested the great majority of these constituencies (37 of the 41), having won 22 of the 41 in the 1971 elections. In 1972, however, the CPM could best the CPI-Congress coalition in only four of these constituencies, and, as mentioned previously, the CPI won a whopping 35 of the 41 with the assistance of Congress.

All available evidence indicates that the alliance with Congress was absolutely crucial to the CPI's successes. Indeed, on the basis of the criteria for vital and helpful transfers developed above, our data reveal that the

that the CPM retained most of the support transferred to it by UF allies in these constituencies. The classification does less well predicting the CPI's fortunes in 1971, mostly because the CPI lost much of its own as well as transferred support in these constituencies.

[45] This statement is based on the fact that Congress was the party which finished second in each constituency in which a vital transfer took place. Except for the transfers, Congress would have won these constituencies and ended up with 71 seats to the CPM's 64. It is also relevant that none of the parties transferring vital support to the CPM (the CPI, Bangla Congress, and Forward Bloc) had been allied with the CPM in 1967.

[46] For the CPI, 6 of 30 wins; for the CPM, 16 of 80.

CPI received transferred support from the Congress in 24 of the 41 constituencies it contested, in 14 of these cases the transferred support being vital to victory and in another nine cases the transferred support being helpful (see Table 19). In addition, the CPI received transferred support from the Bangla Congress in six constituencies (the Bangla Congress having merged with Congress just prior to the 1972 elections), in four of the six such support being vital and in the other two merely helpful. All in all, the CPI was dependent on transferred support from its alliance with Congress in 29 of the 35 constituencies it won, vitally so in 18 constituencies.

That the CPI gained more from the alliance with Congress than the Congress itself did can be seen from figures for CPI transfers to Congress, which are not nearly as impressive. For example, in the 208 constituencies lost by the CPM in 1972, Congress secured vital support from the CPI in only six constituencies, even though it received inconsequential transfers from the CPI in another 14 constituencies. In most constituencies Congress was dependent on transferred votes from the Bangla Congress and the Organization Congress, the major portions of both parties having reassembled under the Congress banner prior to the 1972 elections. CPI assistance to the Congress, then, was of a much smaller magnitude than Congress assistance to the CPI.

From the standpoint of the CPM, of course, the CPI-Congress coalition was damaging, but not nearly as damaging as the merger of the Bangla and

TABLE 19

**The Importance of Transferred Support from Congress to CPI Victories
in 1972**

The Instrumental Value of a Transfer	Constituencies in which the CPI Received Transfers from Congress		
	New Victories	Also Won in 1967	Total: CPI Wins (1972)
	(N)	(N)	((N
Vital	14	—	9
Helpful	9	— ..	14
Inconsequential	—	1 ..	1
Totals ..	23	1 ..	24

Note : A "vital" transfer is one which made the difference between victory and defeat for the CPI in 1972. A "helpful" transfer was not essential to victory but was nevertheless large enough to account for more than a fifth of the gain in the CPI vote. An "inconsequential" transfer amounted to less than a fifth of the growth in CPI support.

Organization Congresses with the New Congress of Mrs. Gandhi. Indeed, if one subtracts the 14 victories that the CPI achieved with vital transfers from the Congress and the six victories that Congress achieved with vital transfers from the CPI, one is still left with 196 Congress victories, all of which are based on factors other than the coalition between Congress and the CPI. This in turn would indicate that the nature of alliances between the Congress and the two CP's is quite important for the CP's themselves, but that exploration of other factors is needed to explain the overall outcome of elections.

Figures for vote transfers also point up the limited extent to which the CPI can expect to act as a "swing" party in electoral alliance-building, at least so long as it is overly dependent on its coalition partners. The 1969 and 1972 elections indicate that the CPI can either help or hurt the CPM to a significant degree, depending on the kinds of coalition it chooses to join, while all four elections support the conclusion that the CPI cannot completely override other factors in its attempts to damage the larger Communist party. In none of the four elections under review has the CPI been able to tilt the balance in favour of one West Bengal party or the other, and yet the portion of statewide support maintained by the CPI is large enough that this could conceivably occur in a very close election in the future. In short, the 1972 results support the view expressed earlier, that the CPI has the potential to act as a swing party in future electoral politics in the state, but that this role would be enhanced if the smaller CP could ever rid itself of its excessive dependence on larger electoral allies.

V. A Summary Assessment

This study has been essentially a portrait of the two Communist parties in West Bengal as participants in electoral politics. Our analysis began with a review of their presence and performance in West Bengal elections, particularly during the past turbulent decade. It then explored trends in the Communist vote over the four elections held between 1967 and 1972 and attempted some rough calculations of the extent to which and the levels at which that vote might be considered institutionalized. Both of these inquiries pointed to the importance of the competitive environment as conditioned by the tactical alignments of the leading parties vis-a-vis one another. In Section IV, accordingly, we looked at the fluid pattern of interactions among the CPI, CPM, and Congress and examined the relative impact on each party of the different alliance arrangements that have existed in West Bengal in recent years.

Our analysis has been almost entirely internal to election data, the broader demographic and economic context in which elections take place being beyond our capacity to handle systematically.[47]   We are therefore not in a position to say who votes for the CP's on the basis of our study or to identify what conditions in society facilitate or impede their electoral fortunes.[48]   Yet we believe we have shown that there is much to be learned from the analysis of election dynamics alone which complements other types of analysis while focusing directly on the electoral environment as the principal determinant of party success.

Our review of the election data has highlighted the limited geographical base of the CPI and CPM in West Bengal, a finding which is notable in two respects.   In the first place, both parties have done remarkably well in spite of their regional confinement, and this is because they have manipulated the party system with consummate skill to amass very much greater power in the state than their own size or appeal would warrant.   Notwithstanding the other types of political action for which Communists are well known, the CP's in West Bengal have shown themselves to be adept players of the electoral game.   At the same time, however, it is clear that there are severe constraints on their capacity for continued growth in the future.

The CPI in particular requires electoral allies in order to gain access to the centers of power, but the only really viable allies left in West Bengal are the CPM and Congress, both of which are larger parties with no interest in having the CPI enter their areas of dominance.   When the CPI tried to go-it-alone in 1971, it suffered doubly; it neither made adequate inroads in the many constituencies it contested for the first time, nor was it immune in those constituencies where it had been contesting all along to the retaliation of parties it offended by its own expanded efforts.   The CPI's limited size and its vulnerability leave it "boxed in" spatially and dependent electorally, a situation that threatens both its prospects for growth and its autonomy.

The CPM is a more potent party than the CPI, but it too occupies a limited electoral base running along the river ways and railroad lines that traverse the centre of the state (an area often referred to as the Calcutta-Durgapur industrial conurbation).   Elsewhere it has contested sporadically

---

[47] For the systematic linking of election with census data, at the district level, see W. H. Morris-Jones and B. Das Gupta, "India's Political Areas: Interim Report on an Ecological Electoral Investigation," *Asian Survey,* June 1969 (Vol. 9), pp. 399-424; and with particular reference to the Communist parties, a provocative study by Donald S. Zagoria, "The Ecology of Peasant Communism in India," *American Political Science Review,* March 1971 (Vol. 65), pp. 144-160.

[48] Needless to say, these are matters concerning which there has been extensive debate. A particularly lucid analysis may be found in Zagoria, *ibid.,* as well as in his earlier study, "The Social Bases of Indian Communism," in Richard Lowenthal (ed.), *Issues in the Future of Asia, Communist and Non-Communist Alternatives* (New York: Praeger, 1969), pp. 97-124.

at best and without much to show for its pains. Even in 1971, when the CPM put up candidates throughout West Bengal and performed so much better than ever before, its victories were still confined largely to the Bengali heartland. And in 1972 it lost heavily even there in the face of a substantially reunited Congress in league with the CPI. Unlike the CPI, the CPM can stand effectively on its own; but when it does so, it can be beaten by a well-consolidated vote against it.

For the CPM, therefore, several future strategies are possible, but all entail risks: it can cultivate allies once again (in which case it must limit its own electoral ambitions); it can pursue an independent strategy (but invite coordinated counteraction); it can attempt to expand its social base of support by mobilizing new elements of the electorate in order to overcome the established strength of its opponents (other parties are trying to do the same thing, of course); and it can reject electoral politics in favour of a more militant posture (which would threaten repression and nullification of the gains already made). That these options are not mutually exclusive affords room for maneuver, but it also serves to accentuate the difficulty of putting together a viable tactical line which will satisfy the different factions of the party. The legacy of its past successes and failures has left the CPM on the horns of a dilemma.

Of course, the fluidity of party politics in West Bengal, combined with the explosive potential of socio-economic conditions in the state, may offer future opportunities to the CP's which can be only dimly perceived at the present time. Yet for all the change that has occurred since 1967, our analysis has revealed at least two respects in which an underlying continuity can be discerned as well. The first has to do with vote trends. Despite substantial, even breathtaking, variation in the number of seats won and lost by the major parties during this period, there has been considerable regularity in the support these parties have received in a fairly substantial number of constituencies. Second, even when the vote for the CPI, CPM, and Congress has fluctuated it has often been possible to relate the fluctuation to transfers from allies. Elections in West Bengal are not random exercises. Knowing how well a party has done in a previous election tells us something— at times a great deal—about its probable strength (or that of an ally) in a subsequent election. Our data on the regularity of vote trends and the predictability of vote transfers can be read either as not much to boast about or as impressive magnitudes of continuity, depending on one's initial expectations and one's assessment of our criteria for evaluation (which we feel to be reasonable, if strict).

Finally, it is difficult to extrapolate from what has been essentially a descriptive study to the broader theoretical concerns of comparative scholarship. We did not set out to test any theories in this exercise, and what we have learned has only tangential relevance to such academic topics as patterns of change, system institutionalization, and the like. Even so, much of what we have documented here illustrates the extent to which radicalism in West Bengal (and India as a whole) has been harnessed to the democratic process, notwithstanding objective miseries and subjective grievances. Although other factors disposing in this direction are surely at work—we have noted the contribution of India's size and heterogeneity, for example—the absorption of Indian Communism into the democratic system says something about the socializing potential of electoral politics generally and the vitality of the Indian political process in particular. Elections have become the fulcrum of Indian political life: the principal expression of unity in diversity, of conflict and cohesion, continuity and change, and of institutional order despite far-reaching social and economic reorientation. Whether this will continue to be true if the serious conditions within West Bengal worsen or become characteristic of other parts of India as well is a troubling question, but one which lies well beyond our data and competence to answer.

APPENDIX

APPENDIX

CONSTITUENCY-BY-CONSTITUENCY DISTRIBUTION OF THE VOTE FOR ALL ELECTIONS IN WEST BENGAL (1952-1972)

This appendix contains a list of all of the constituencies in West Bengal for the seven elections to the state legislative assembly held between 1952 and 1972. The numbers which appear before the names of the constituencies are the numbers that were used by the Election Commission in their official *Report* for 1967, and these will coincide exactly with the numbers used by the Election Commission for the 1969, 1971, and 1972 elections. Since Indian constituency boundaries (and numbers) are changed after each census, the constituencies that were contested in 1957 and 1962 will differ somewhat from those for 1967-72; and the constituencies used in 1952 will again be somewhat different. The 1952 constituencies were based on the 1941 census, the 1957 and 1962 constituencies were based on the 1951 census, and the 1967-72 constituencies were based on the 1961 census. Constituency names that were used in the elections prior to 1967, but have not been used since, have been listed in the tables as "others." Wherever possible we have attempted to identify constituency equivalents (i.e., those constituencies that did not change significantly over time) and where this could be done we have noted the different names of approximately equivalent constituencies in the margins of the tables.

The tables list the percentage of the vote received by the candidates of the various political parties that contested the seven elections in West Bengal thus far, the data for these tables being derived from the official *Reports* of the Election Commission. Since the Election Commission listed some of the smaller Marxist-left parties in West Bengal as independents in the 1957 and 1962 elections, it was necessary to check party lists of candidate for these years to determine the candidates of some of the smaller parties.

Mention should also be made of the manner in which party votes are listed for the double-member constituencies that were used in 1952 and 1957. In double-member constituencies each of the parties was permitted the option of offering two candidates in one constituency, one candidate for each of the seats being contested in that constituency. For this reason the figures (1) and (2) will appear behind the names of the parties in those instances when the parties ran two candidates in a double-member constituency. It should also be pointed out that the votes received by the Socialist Party and the Kisan Mazdoor Praja Party (KMPP) in the 1952 elections are listed under the Praja Socialist Party (PSP), since these two parties merged to form the PSP immediately after the 1952 elections and remained together until the PSP itself merged with the SSP to form the Socialist Party in 1972. This means that the PSP will occasionally have two candidates listed in single-member constituencies and as many as four candidates in double-member constituencies for the 1952 elections (these being instances in which both the KMPP and Socialist parties offered candidates in 1952).

In the tables the percentage of the vote received by the winning candidate (*or candidates*) has been indicated in bold type so as to more readily identify the winning party. A list of abbreviations used for the various parties listed in the tables appears on the following page.

ABBREVIATIONS

BBC—Biplabi Bangla Congress
BJD—Bangla Jatiya Dal
BKD—Bharatya Kranti Dal
BNP—Bengal National Party
CPI—Communist Party of India
CPM—Communist Party of India-Marxist
HMS—Hindu Mahasabha
INDF—Indian National Democratic Front
NPB—National Party of Bengal
PML—Progressive Muslim League
PSP—Praja Socialist Party
RCPI—Revolutionary Communist Party of India
RPI—Revolutionary Party of India
RRP—Ram Rajya Parishad
RSP—Revolutionary Socialist Party
SBP—Samyukta Biplabi Parishad
SSP—Samyukta Socialist Party
SUC—Socialist Unity Centre

COOCH-BEHAR DISTRICT	1. MEKLIGANJ							2. MATHABHANGA						
	1952	1957	1962	1967	1969	1971	1972	1952	1957	1962	1967	1969	1971	1972
Congress	45.7	43.5	36.3	34.2	46.5	35.3	57.7	73.5	54.6	55.0	35.7	51.5	45.1	60.2
Congress (O)					8.3								4.7	
Bangla Congress													3.0	
CPI										45.0				
CPM					8.8					64.3	48.5	38.9	39.8	
Forward Bloc		32.1	63.7	64.0	52.4	43.9	40.8						5.4	
Proutist				1.1										
HMS		3.8												
Swatantra			1.8											
Independents	42.3	15.3				3.7	1.5	12.2	45.4				3.1	
	12.0	5.4						8.0						
								6.4						

COOCH-BEHAR DISTRICT	3. COOCH BEHAR WEST							4. SITAI (from DINHATA)						
	1952	1957	1962	1967	1969	1971	1972	1952	1957	1962	1967	1969	1971	1972
Congress			42.5	52.7	45.2	68.6				34.8	49.0	60.1	44.7	65.1
Congress (O)						14.1							19.9	
CPM						27.5							9.2	
Forward Bloc				35.5	43.2	13.2	31.4			46.4	45.8	40.0	26.1	34.9
Lok Dal					2.7									
Jana Sangh					1.4									
Swatantra				22.0								5.2		
Independents								18.8						

(See Dinhata)

Cooch-Behar District	5. Dinhata							6. Cooch Behar North						
	1952	1957	1962	1967	1969	1971	1972	1952	1957	1962	1967	1969	1971	1972
Congress (1)	**33.0**	**31.2**	37.2	43.5	**53.5**	**45.1**	**58.5**		37.5	**37.7**	46.1		**49.6**	**58.8**
Congress (2)	**33.8**	**24.6**												
Congress (O)					5.1								2.1	1.1
Bangla Congress													1.1	
CPI	7.6													
CPM						9.2					19.3		34.7	
Forward Bloc (1)	8.6	18.2	**60.9**	**55.0**	44.1	40.6	39.9			**62.5**	33.1	**51.0**	12.6	40.1
Forward Bolc (2)		16.3												
PSP	3.8													
Lok Dal												1.3		
Proutist				1.6								1.2		
Jana Sangh												0.5		
Swatantra			1.5								9.9			
Independents	13.2	4.2	1.9	0.9	1.6									
		5.4												

Cooch-Behar District	7. Cooch Behar South							8. Tufanganj						
	1952	1957	1962	1967	1969	1971	1972	1952	1957	1962	1967	1969	1971	1972
Congress			33.6	**42.7**	**54.0**	**43.6**	**62.9**	**64.4**	41.4	**55.7**	**59.1**		**52.3**	**67.8**
Congress (O)					6.4								4.6	
Bangla Congress					3.1									
CPI								29.2	**52.4**	5.5				
CPM				13.0	30.3	36.5					24.1	39.0	34.2	32.7
Forward Bloc			**57.8**	32.4	45.0	16.7							8.4	
Lok Dal				1.0								1.9		
Swatantra										14.7				
Independents			8.6	8.7	0.6			6.4	4.2					
				1.7					2.0					
				1.5										

Others : Cooch Behar

COOCH-BEHAR DISTRICT	1952	1957	1962	1967	1969	1971	1972
Congress (1)	**27.8**	**24.9**					
Congress (2)	**25.7**	**23.5**	(See				
CPI	11.0	20.1	Cooch				
CPM			Behar				
Forward Bloc	13.1	18.5	North, and				
PSP (1)	3.2		South)				
PSP (2)	2.8						
PSP (3)	3.2						
Independents	4.4	8.9					
	3.0	4.1					
	2.4						
	2.0						
	1.6						

JALPAIGURI DISTRICT	9. KUMARGRAM							10. KALCHINI						
	1952	1957	1962	1967	1969	1971	1972	1952	1957	1962	1967	1969	1971	1972
Congress (1)				**41.3**	**48.2**	**43.9**	**69.7**	**28.3**	38.5	**51.1**	**63.2**	**38.8**	**51.5**	
Congress (2)	(See							**23.6**						
Congress (O)	Alipurduars)					10.8							1.3	
CPM			23.1	34.4	21.1	30.3								
Forward Bloc			7.7			8.6							8.1	
RSP						10.7		17.2	**43.5**		35.6	31.7	37.8	
PSP								13.8	4.9					
INDF				10.9										
Proutist					**1.8**									
Independents			22.9	**4.6**		2.6		12.2	7.4	39.2	1.2	18.7	10.7	
			5.0			2.1		4.9	4.5	8.6		1.3		
										1.3	1.2			

JALPAIGURI DISTRICT	11. ALIPURDUARS							12. FALAKATA						
	1952	1957	1962	1967	1969	1971	1972	1952	1957	1962	1967	1969	1971	1972
Congress (1)	*	**49.2**	**50.1**	42.7	47.4	**41.8**	**55.6**	46.4	**40.4**	32.6	**58.9**		**33.0**	**64.2**
Congress (2)	66.7													
Congress (O)													4.0	
Bangla Congress			3.8		1.7									
CPI									17.0					
CPM					22.9								28.1	
Forward Bloc	6.4													
RSP	26.9	34.2	43.6	**53.5**	**51.3**	22.5	42.5						5.9	
PSP		2.0						**47.3**	37.0	**38.8**	4.5		3.2	
SSP					1.9						28.6	28.2	12.0	
Proutist				1.4								4.2		
Socialist														35.8
Independents		13.5	4.3			1.8	1.9	6.4	5.6				4.2	10.6
		3.1				1.4								3.2

*Won unopposed

JALPAIGURI DISTRICT	13. MADARIHAT							14. DHUPGURI						
	1952	1957	1962	1967	1969	1971	1972	1952	1957	1962	1967	1969	1971	1972
Congress		38.0	**42.7**	44.3	20.4	35.6	**57.3**				32.1	45.5	**29.0**	**57.4**
Congress (O)					3.2								2.2	
Bangla Congress								(See Fala-Kata)				7.9	3.5	
CPM					7.9									17.9
Forward Bloc							12.7							
RSP			**38.3**	38.3	**46.1**	**33.1**	43.7							1.7
PSP			16.0			27.2					**47.1**			
SSP					9.3							**49.2**	28.5	
INDF												4.5		
Lok Dal				9.6										
Socialist														35.0
Independents			4.6	12.3	24.6	20.7	2.9				6.6	0.9	13.5	5.9
			3.1	6.7	1.5						4.1		3.6	1.8
											2.1			

JALPAIGURI DISTRICT

	15. NAGRAKATA							16. MAINAGURI						
	1952	1957	1962	1967	1969	1971	1972	1952	1957	1962	1967	1969	1971	1972
Congress		**46.6**	**48.3**	**48.6**	24.2			62.7	51.9	37.7	30.7	**44.3**	**35.0**	56.5
Congress (O)						1.6							3.4	
Bangla Congress											35.9	19.2	9.2	
CPI		29.3				57.2				16.4			6.4	
CPM			33.0	40.2	57.8	38.6							10.5	
PSP		15.0			6.4	12.6		37.3	33.3	25.7	31.8	32.1	4.8	
RSP													14.1	23.8
INDF				0.8								0.8		
Jana Sangh											1.3	2.3		
Independents		7.2	18.7	3.9	3.9	4.3		8.7	17.6	0.3	1.3	16.6	19.7	
		1.9						6.2	2.6					

JALPAIGURI DISTRICT

	17. MAL							18. JALPAIGURI						
	1952	1957	1962	1967	1969	1971	1972	1952	1957	1962	1967	1969	1971	1972
Congress (1)	19.4	**51.8**	**54.3**	**57.0**	**32.7**	**61.8**		**27.4**	**26.4**	**48.7**	**42.0**	46.0	**49.9**	**64.2**
Congress (2)	22.9							31.9	26.9					
Congress (O)					2.1								1.9	
Bangla Congress													1.5	
CPI (1)	**21.8**	26.5	26.1	30.4	22.0			14.7	23.3	31.8	28.8	51.2	14.7	
CPI (2)								8.6						
CPM						23.3	38.2				27.2		28.3	35.8
PSP (1)	21.8	21.7	19.6	10.9	8.2			7.9	16.7	8.5				
PSP (2)								6.0						
RSP					7.5									
INDF					0.8									
Lok Dal					1.0									
Jana Sangh												1.9		
Independents	8.2					4.2		3.5	3.5	11.0	2.0	1.0	3.8	
	3.4							3.2						
	2.6													

JALPAIGURI DISTRICT	19. RAJGANJ							Others : KHARIA						
	1952	1957	1962	1967	1969	1971	1972	1952	1957	1962	1967	1969	1971	1972
Congress				36.4	**55.6**	**35.3**	**59.3**		**50.6**					
Congress (O)						9.1				(See				
Bangla Congress				24.6		4.1						Rajganj)		
CPI									32.2					
CPM						**30.9**	**31.2**							
SSP				**39.1**	36.5	12.3								
Socialist							9.6							
Lok Dal					4.0									
Independents					3.9	8.3			11.1					
									5.6					
									0.5					

JALPAIGURI DISTRICT	Others : WESTERN DUARS							Others : CENTRAL DUARS						
	1952	1957	1962	1967	1969	1971	1972	1952	1957	1962	1967	1969	1971	1972
Congress (1)	**28.2**							**26.5**						
Congress (2)	**28.6**							**19.9**						
PSP (1)	10.7		(See Mal)					10.0		(See Falakata)				
PSP (2)	13.3							13.1						
PSP (3)	11.1													
PSP (4)	8.2													
Independents								15.9						
								7.0						
								6.0						
								1.7						

DARJEELING DISTRICT	20. KALIMPONG							21. DARJEELING						
	1952	1957	1962	1967	1969	1971	1972	1952	1957	1962	1967	1969	1971	1972
Congress	40.1		31.8	**50.7**	40.0	17.1	37.6	26.1	21.5	18.4	32.5	42.3	28.4	22.3
CPI	**59.9**		8.3	5.0				25.9	32.2	24.8				
CPM						16.6	12.3						25.0	
PSP		10.6	1.3								1.3			
Jana Sangh				4.0	2.9									
Gurkha League		**49.1**	**51.2**	40.4	**55.1**	2.2	32.5	**48.1**	33.3	**49.1**	**51.0**	**57.7**	**46.6**	**45.3**
Independents		33.6	2.9		2.3	**38.1**	17.6		5.9	6.5	16.5			28.8
		5.0	0.7			26.0			4.1					2.4
		1.8	0.4						3.1					1.2
			0.2											

DARJEELING DISTRICT	22. JOREBUNGALOW							23. KURSEONG-SILLIGURI						
	1952	1957	1962	1967	1969	1971	1972	1952	1957	1962	1967	1969	1971	1972
Congress (1)	15.4	23.1	17.2	36.3	41.4	19.0	32.6	**15.3**	**15.7**	**38.2**	32.8	38.8	**50.6**	**65.4**
Congress (2)								16.1	16.0					
Congress (O)						4.7								
Bangla Congress											18.8			
CPI (1)	20.2	**32.5**	**41.7**					13.0	**17.5**	32.7			13.8	
CPI (2)									14.3					
CPM				20.7		**38.6**	31.2				15.4		29.9	29.9
PSP (1)								11.7						
PSP (2)								3.1						
PSP (3)								2.3						
Proutist												**1.2**		
Jana Sangh									2.9		5.2	**2.7**		
Gurkha League (1)	**64.4**	26.5	41.0	**43.0**	**58.6**	37.7	**34.1**	**16.7**	11.8	22.4	26.2	**57.3**	3.3	
Gurkha League (2)								13.9	7.5					
Independents		8.7					2.1	5.5	7.2	6.7	1.7		2.5	3.2
		5.8						2.4	3.8					1.5
		3.4							3.2					

DARJEELING DISTRICTS — 24. PHANSIDEWA

	1952	1957	1962	1967	1969	1971	1972	1952
Congress			**41.9**	**45.4**	**53.4**	**43.8**	**62.3**	
Congress (O)		(See				4.1		
Bangla Congress		Kurseong-				4.9		
CPI		Silliguri)	36.8					
CPM				29.3	28.6	33.4	37.7	
Forward Bloc						7.8		
RSP						4.5		
Proutist					1.0			
Jana Sangh					2.5			
Gurkha League		21.3	25.3					
Independents					9.2	1.6		
					5.3			

WEST DINAJPUR DISTRICT — 25. CHOPRA / 26. GOALPOKHAR

	25. CHOPRA							26. GOALPOKHAR						
	1952	1957	1962	1967	1969	1971	1972	1952	1957	1962	1967	1969	1971	1972
Congress	*		**47.8**	**24.9**	**21.7**	**39.8**	**63.1**		**57.3**	38.6	13.9	22.7	**34.7**	**54.2**
Congress (O)						3.0							3.8	
Bangla Congress						2.3							13.1	
CPI			21.3	8.1										
CPM				21.9	27.9	32.3	36.2						5.4	
Forward Bloc					10.5					6.0	11.5			
PSP			1.3	7.4	1.6	0.8		42.7	**41.4**	**36.5**	**45.5**	4.9		
SSP										31.3	5.5	5.0		
Lok Dal											0.9			
Socialist							0.8							9.2
INDF											17.6			
Proutist				4.8							1.5			
Swatantra	13.0								14.0	2.1				
HMS											6.2			
Muslim League														36.6
Independents			13.9	21.1	**44.0**	11.2				4.6	29.8			
			2.5	13.6							3.3			
			0.3	3.0										

*Won unopposed

WEST DINAJPUR DISTRICT	27. KARANDIGHI							28. RAIGANJ						
	1952	1957	1962	1967	1969	1971	1972	1952	1957	1962	1967	1969	1971	1972
Congress (1)	**57.5**	**45.1**	16.8	16.7	**47.0**	**48.9**		**31.2**	**24.7**	**39.1**	30.9	42.9	**48.4**	**65.8**
Congress (2)								30.0	23.3					
Congress (O)					8.2								2.7	
CPI								8.3	15.1	24.6				
CPM					12.8						18.0	**43.0**	44.3	31.2
Forward Bloc (1)		7.0	24.5	**37.5**	25.8			14.6						
Forward Bloc (2)								13.1						
PSP	32.2	38.5	**38.6**	4.3	1.8				22.6	19.9	**41.4**	12.4	4.5	
SSP		9.7												
Socialist					3.6									2.0
INDF				35.3								0.9		
Proutist					1.8							0.8		
Swatantra		5.0								0.3				
Independents	10.3	2.0	8.6	4.5	2.8	44.3		2.9	14.3	13.0	5.4			0.7
		2.4	1.9		1.7	1.8				3.1	4.3			0.4
					1.4									

WEST DINAJPUR DISTRICT	29. KALIAGANJ							30. ITAHAR						
	1952	1957	1962	1967	1969	1971	1972	1952	1957	1962	1967	1969	1971	1972
Congress			**39.0**	**42.1**	**54.9**	**55.5**	**68.4**	**47.2**	32.9	**52.5**	**55.4**	**51.0**	**59.2**	**78.2**
Congress (O)						4.2	3.0						3.8	
Bangla Congress				9.8		3.5					2.7			
CPI			30.0			7.6		24.2	**34.6**	45.8		47.1	12.4	
CPM				39.8	44.4	29.3	27.3						24.6	21.8
Forward Bloc								24.4						
PSP			7.0											
Socialist							1.4							
INDF					0.7							0.7		
Proutist												1.2		
Swatantra			24.0											
Independents				6.0				4.3	22.2	1.7	22.8			
				2.4					5.9		15.3			
									2.5		3.9			
									1.9					

	31. Kushmandi							32. Gangarampur						
West Dinajpur District	1952	1957	1962	1967	1969	1971	1972	1952	1957	1962	1967	1969	1971	1972
Congress (1)		30.1	40.2	50.1	52.9	76.5	49.3	19.0	42.7	26.7	43.7		56.5	70.5
Congress (2)								22.0						
Congress (O)					14.1									
Bangla Congress													8.7	
CPI		42.1	21.3	49.1	18.8				50.2	20.2				
CPM					11.6					20.6	48.0		28.3	28.3
RSP						12.8	23.5						5.8	
PSP		16.5						19.7	13.0	5.1				
RCPI								19.7					0.8	
INDF				0.8								2.2		
Lok Dal												3.3		
Proutist												2.1		
Swatantra		11.2									2.0			
Independents			18.7; 18.0; 1.8					4.4; 3.6; 3.3; 4.7; 3.2; 3.1	15.0; 14.1; 5.9			12.8; 11.1; 8.6	0.8	**1.2**

	33. Kumarganj							34. Balurghat						
West Dinajpur District	1952	1957	1962	1967	1969	1971	1972	1952	1957	1962	1967	1969	1971	1972
Congress (1)				46.2	38.6	38.6	59.6	31.2	20.3	49.8	41.5	36.2	46.1	54.1
Congress (2)								28.0	21.2					
Bangla Congress	(See			22.7	45.8	8.2								
CPI	Ganga-				5.0								7.3	
CPM	Rampur)			20.9		35.7	40.4							
Forward Bloc (1)								3.3						
Forward Bloc (2)								1.9						
Lok Dal					8.3									
RSP (1)					12.6			13.0	23.2	46.0	50.6	56.7	42.1	44.0
RSP (2)								11.6	19.5					
PSP										4.2		1.4		
INDF					1.7							0.7		
Proutist												0.3		0.7
Jana Sangh				5.6								4.7	2.6	
Independents				10.2				7.3; 3.7; 3.0; 2.6; 1.6	4.8; 3.8	5.9; 1.5; 0.6			1.7; 0.2	0.7; 0.4

WEST DINAJPUR DISTRICT — 35. TAPAN

Party	1952	1957	1962	1967	1969	1971	1972
Congress			41.5	36.2	47.4	**42.5**	**58.0**
Congress (O)						1.5	
CPI						6.0	
CPM						14.4	
RSP			**52.9**	**58.0**	**51.3**	35.7	**41.2**
INDF					**1.3**		
Independents			5.6	5.8			**0.8**

MALDA DISTRICT — 36. HABIBPUR   /   37. GAJOL

Party	H 1952	H 1957	H 1962	H 1967	H 1969	H 1971	H 1972	G 1952	G 1957	G 1962	G 1967	G 1969	G 1971	G 1972
Congress	36.0	**47.5**	47.0	15.6		38.3				**56.3**	52.1			**60.1**
Congress (O)					31.1			(See				12.1		
Bangla Congress					5.1			Malda)				34.3		
CPI	**58.8**	46.1	**47.1**	13.9		**60.4**	44.7			9.7		9.0		
CPM					29.5					28.7	40.6	**44.6**	33.5	
Jana Sangh	5.2		5.8								7.3		6.4	
Swatantra		6.4								5.3				
Independents				10.1 / 6.5 / 5.4 / 2.7 / 2.5	34.3									

MALDA DISTRICT — 38. KHARBA   /   39. HARISHCHANDRAPUR

Party	K 1952	K 1957	K 1962	K 1967	K 1969	K 1971	K 1972	H 1952	H 1957	H 1967	H 1967	H 1969	H 1971	H 1972
Congress	**64.8**	40.0	37.2	43.4	41.2	41.9	**47.8**	**58.7**	22.9	**55.3**	40.8	49.8	2.9	**50.7**
Congress (O)						1.4	5.8						40.0	3.0
Bangla Congress						1.1							0.5	
CPI	26.1													
CPM						**53.7**	46.5							
PSP	9.1							35.3	25.7					
Worker's Party									51.4	44.7	**56.3**	**50.2**	**54.3**	46.3
Jana Sangh				4.5										
Swatantra											0.8			
Independents		**54.1** / 5.9	**56.8** / 6.9	**56.6**	**54.3**	1.9		5.9			2.2		2.3	

MALDA DISTRICT	40. RATUA							41. MALDA						
	1952	1957	1962	1967	1969	1971	1972	1952	1957	1962	1967	1969	1971	1972
Congress (1)	**76.3**	**25.8**	**52.2**	**40.8**	45.4	**43.0**	**52.8**	**21.1**	26.9	29.9	**49.2**	**55.9**	**39.9**	**62.7**
Congress (2)	**22.2**							20.4	**30.2**					
Congress (O)					6.5								7.8	
Bangla Congress			10.0		1.4						6.6	39.1	3.6	
CPI (1)		9.0			5.8			20.5	23.5	**52.3**			14.5	
CPI (2)									19.4					
CPM						41.5	45.3						27.6	37.3
PSP	16.5													
INDF				3.6										
Jana Sangh											2.8			
HMS								10.7						
Swatantra			17.0	17.5							22.5	5.0		
Independents	7.2	16.4	14.5	31.6	**51.0**	1.8	1.8	**22.0**			13.8	17.1		6.6
		11.2	9.5					5.3			1.2	4.7		
		8.2	6.8											
		4.8												
		2.4												

MALDA DISTRICT	42. ENGLISHBAZAR							43. MANIKCHAK						
	1952	1957	1962	1967	1969	1971	1972	1952	1957	1962	1967	1969	1971	1972
Congress	**49.2**	**41.0**	**32.6**	32.0	17.2		36.1	50.0	26.1	**42.4**	**37.3**			**58.5**
Congress (O)													8.3	
CPI		34.9	24.9	**54.8**	**31.6**	54.9				47.0	11.4	42.0	25.4	
CPM			18.2		22.7	31.2							29.0	41.5
PSP							13.2				(See Ratua)			
INDF				1.5										
Jana Sangh		15.9	15.0	11.8	26.7	13.8								
Swatantra			3.9								**50.3**	15.7		
Independents			34.0	5.4		1.8	28.4			2.0	7.7			
			17.3				8.9			1.1	4.5			
			7.7				7.7							
							5.7							

MALDA DISTRICT	44. SUZAPUR							45. KALIACHAK						
	1952	1957	1962	1967	1969	1971	1972	1952	1957	1962	1967	1969	1971	1972
Congress	29.4	**62.0**	**75.5**	**70.4**	**60.4**	**70.1**			**50.7**	34.2	30.9	**35.5**	**36.0**	**43.4**
Congress (O)					15.5									
Bangla Congress			6.5	21.9							14.8			
CPI										9.7				
CPM											**41.7**	15.9	25.2	
Forward Bloc													7.9	
RSP													28.9	13.5
INDF				7.8							14.4			
Jana Sangh												8.0		
Swatantra			38.0	8.4							12.6	0.3		
Muslim League						9.9								
Independents		**37.1**		4.1		15.6	20.1	37.7	**48.1**			25.9	2.1	43.1
		33.5		3.7		8.5		5.5	3.5					
			1.9					2.5	3.5					
								1.9	0.5					
								1.7						

(See Kaliachk North and South)

MALDA DISTRICT	*Others:* KALIACHAK NORTH							*Others:* KALIACHAK SOUTH						
	1952	1957	1962	1967	1969	1971	1972	1952	1957	1962	1967	1969	1971	1972
Congress	44.0	(See Kaliachak)						**51.2**	(See Kaliachak)					
RSP								38.1						
Independents	**56.0**							10.7						

MURSHIDABAD DISTRICT	46. FARAKKA							47. SUTI						
	1952	1957	1962	1967	1969	1971	1972	1952	1957	1962	1967	1969	1971	1972
Congress	**48.6**	**47.0**	**47.0**	22.8	17.9	16.2	40.6	31.2	**51.0**	**56.1**	45.8	**50.3**	**38.1**	46.5
Congress (O)					2.1									
Bangla Congress				**59.6**	**31.8**	2.5								
CPM						38.6	44.1							
RSP								31.6	45.0	43.9	**54.2**	49.7	32.2	**49.2**
PSP								14.4	2.0					
Jana Sangh					17.0									
Swatantra			27.0		0.7									
PML					30.2									
SUC						3.9								4.5
Independents	24.2	34.0	18.7	9.1	2.4	36.2	15.4	21.9	2.0				11.0	4.3
	19.9	13.0	4.4	8.6								1.0	10.0	
	5.1	6.1	2.9										2.8	
	2.2												0.9	
													0.6	

Murshadabad District

	48. Jangipur							49. Sagardighi						
	1952	1957	1962	1967	1969	1971	1972	1952	1957	1962	1967	1969	1971	1972
Congress (1)	**17.0**	**37.5**	37.4	45.9	25.4	**42.3**	**16.0**	(See Jangipur)	**61.1**	**49.9**	**40.0**		29.1	**56.7**
Congress (2)	**21.0**						16.4							
Congress (O)					4.8								1.3	
Bangla Congress										42.9	**60.0**		14.9	
RSP	14.0	32.8	**62.6**	**51.3**	17.9								22.2	36.8
SUC					15.4	35.5								
PSP (1)	8.0								11.4					
PSP (2)	10.0													
Jana Sangh				2.9			1.0							
BBC													14.2	
Independents	8.1	16.6			**27.1**	12.0	12.5		19.8	7.2			15.9	6.4
	6.0	13.1			4.4	10.2	7.9		7.0				2.5	
	4.1				3.3		7.3		0.6					
	3.2				1.6		4.8		0.1					
	2.9						4.6							
	2.6						4.3							
	2.1						4.0							
	1.0						2.5							
							2.3							
							1.7							
							0.9							
							0.6							
							0.5							
							0.4							

Murishidabad District

	50. Lalgola							51. Bhagabangola						
	1952	1967	1962	1967	1969	1971	1972	1952	1957	1962	1967	1969	1971	1972
Congress	**67.2**	**50.1**	**56.9**	**69.2**	**59.9**	**44.2**	**59.6**		**42.5**	38.8	**43.5**	36.0	19.3	**63.1**
Congress (O)					2.7									
Bangla Congress													2.7	
CPM						31.8								
PSP	5.0								34.3	**55.1**				
SSP											36.8	**37.3**	6.4	
Socialist														15.2
Forward Bloc	1.2													
Jana Sangh				2.0									20.0	8.4
PML					6.8							22.7		
BJD												3.1		
Muslim League														13.3
Independents	25.8	46.2	43.1	25.8	31.4	28.2	6.6		23.2	6.1	13.4	0.9	32.7	
	0.9	3.7		5.0		23.4	2.0				6.3		12.2	
					4.5								7.0	

MURSHIDABAD DISTRICT	52. NABAGRAM							53. MURSHIDABAD						
	1952	1957	1962	1967	1969	1971	1972	1952	1957	1962	1967	1969	1971	1972
Congress	(See Bhagabangola)		**48.0**	38.7	29.4	**50.6**	**60.0**	**49.4**	32.1	**53.1**	39.8		29.3	**50.7**
Congress (O)						5.9	0.9						1.0	
CPM													27.1	39.4
RSP					6.0									
PSP							31.9							
INDF											1.7			
Jana Sangh						1.8					11.4		12.7	3.4
PML											12.4			
BJD				2.7										
Independents			47.3	**58.6**	**55.0**	44.9	8.1	46.4	**50.5**	35.5	34.6		19.1	6.5
			2.4			3.8	1.8	4.2	12.0	5.2			10.8	
			2.4							2.9	4.1			
										2.5	2.0			

MURSHIDABAD DISTRICT	54. JALANGI							55. DOMKAL						
	1952	1957	1962	1967	1969	1971	1972	1952	1957	1962	1967	1969	1971	1972
Congress	**55.1**	**35.0**	33.0	**40.2**	**41.1**	16.6	**42.5**	(See Raninagar)			39.4	**43.1**	17.6	**48.6**
Congress (O)							5.2							
CPM				10.7		17.7	40.1				**60.6**	42.6	**41.1**	47.2
INDF					5.2									
Jana Sangh				12.4	26.4	**33.0**	7.8						3.3	2.2
PML													11.1	
SUC													10.4	
Independents	27.5	30.0	**53.0**	22.2	27.3	32.7	4.4						28.7	4.2
	15.1	21.0	7.0	9.7										
	2.4	14.0	3.4	4.9										
			2.5											
			1.1											

MURSHIDABAD DISTRICT	56. NAODA							57. HARIHARPARA						
	1952	1957	1962	1967	1969	1971	1972	1952	1957	1962	1967	1969	1971	1972
Congress	20.7	**55.0**	**36.1**	**47.5**	19.2	6.0	28.4	**54.9**	**65.0**	**48.1**	**44.2**	18.0	9.9	39.2
Bangla Congress												25.2		
CPM					6.2								10.7	
RSP	**26.1**	26.0	23.7		37.7	12.5	32.6							
INDF												1.6		
BKD				2.1										
Jana Sangh					27.8	3.2							22.1	4.1
PML				**40.9**							**55.2**			
SUC														**45.0**
Muslim League														11.7
Independents	23.3	18.0	17.9	47.1	0.2	**47.5**	**34.4**	21.6	35.0	37.0	37.0		**57.4**	
	19.9	1.0	15.2			1.4		16.6	10.3	10.5				
	10.1		7.1					6.9	2.7	8.3				
									1.6					
									0.3					

MURSHIDABAD DISTRICT	58. BERHAMPORE							59. BELDANGA						
	1952	1957	1962	1967	1969	1971	1972	1952	1957	1962	1967	1969	1971	1972
Congress	**45.9**	**45.5**	39.6	**39.5**	22.9	**44.3**	**68.2**	**32.5**	**45.0**	8.8	**58.2**	9.8		37.1
Congress (O)						2.3								
CPI		42.5	**53.3**	16.9	**48.7**	8.5		9.1						
CPM				19.3	19.7									
Forward Bloc										16.0				
PSP	3.8													
RSP	39.2					14.4	31.8	19.5	36.0	**45.8**		43.4	**42.4**	**40.4**
Jana Sang				5.7								,1.6	3.8	2.3
HMS								28.0	2.0					
PML				10.8										
BJD				11.9										
Independents	11.1	12.0	5.1	22.7		10.8	11.0	0.9	38.8	37.3	**45.2**	26.0	20.2	
			1.2	1.7					4.4	3.4	0.5	23.5		
			0.8						2.2	1.1			4.3	

MURSHIDABAD DISTRICT	60. KANDI							61. KHARGRAM						
	1952	1957	1962	1967	1969	1971	1972	1952	1957	1962	1967	1969	1971	1972
Congress (1)	**38.3**	**29.5**	**50.2**	**60.4**	29.5	**38.4**	**70.6**	**23.7**	(See Kandi)	49.0	**50.5**	30.9	**26.7**	**64.1**
Congress (2)		**31.6**						18.0						
Congress (O)													2.7	
Bangla Congress													5.8	
CPI						8.4							12.6	
CPM						18.1	29.5						26.6	36.0
PSP (1)	13.8							13.6						
PSP (2)								8.2						
RSP	25.2	20.5	49.8	25.8	26.3	10.7		18.3		**51.0**	49.6	**54.2**	12.1	
Jana Sangh					1.4	3.6								
HMS	3.2							5.6						
Lok Dal												4.9		
PML					5.0							10.1		
Independents	9.0	16.8		10.0	**37.8**	20.9		10.2					13.5	
	6.0	1.6		3.9				2.6						
	4.5													

MURSHIDABAD DISTRICT	62. BARWAN							63. BHARATPUR						
	1952	1957	1962	1967	1969	1971	1972	1952	1957	1962	1967	1969	1971	1972
Congress	(See Khargram)	(See Kandi)	42.6	35.4	**42.0**	**59.1**	33.7	52.5	30.0	**31.9**	32.3	24.5		55.9
Congress (O)					1.3								0.7	
Bangla Congress													3.4	
CPM													35.4	42.8
RSP			**47.7**	**45.3**	25.7	40.9	20.8	40.0	**47.4**	29.0	**43.6**	19.0		0.4
SUC										1.6				
INDF					0.6									
Lok Dal					10.2							6.0		
Jana Sangh					1.0	2.0								
PML					3.8									
Independents				9.7	1.0	14.6		17.4	7.5	16.0	24.8	18.1	17.0	1.0
						12.3		12.2		5.1	9.5			
						2.2		8.0			4.8			
								4.5						
								3.6						

MURSHIDABAD DISTRICT	*Others :* RANINAGAR						
	1952	1957	1962	1967	1969	1971	1972
Congress	**61.9**	18.8	18.9				
Independents	25.7	**64.4**	**69.8**	(Sea			
	9.9	7.6	7.0		Domkal)		
	2.6	6.8	4.3				
		2.5					

NADIA DISTRICT	64. KARIMPUR							65. TEHATTA						
	1952	1957	1962	1967	1969	1971	1972	1952	1957	1962	1967	1969	1971	1972
Congress	41.9	**56.0**	**47.0**	22.4	**33.7**	23.6	**61.0**	48.2	**71.0**	56.7	44.4	52.2	21.4	**58.2**
Congress (O)					2.7								5.3	
Bangla Congress			**69.0**		5.7								5.5	
CPI										30.7				
CPM					33.6	**47.6**	35.5				43.3	44.9	**46.5**	40.0
PSP	**48.4**	11.0						16.5	29.0					
Proutist					2.6							2.9		
Jana Sangh			5.0								2.4			
SBP										10.0				
Independents	6.7	19.0	40.0	8.7	30.0	20.4	3.6	28.2		10.0			2.7	1.8
	3.0	9.0	8.0					3.6		2.6			18.7	
		3.3						3.5						
		1.7												

NADIA DISTRICT	66. KALIGANJ							67. NAKASHIPARA						
	1952	1957	1962	1967	1969	1971	1972	1952	1957	1962	1967	1969	1971	1972
Congress (1)	**58.1**		**53.2**	**51.7**	13.0	**41.2**		**45.7**	40.0	**53.4**	38.6	**53.8**	20.7	**55.1**
Congress (2)		(See							**39.0**					
Congress (O)		Nakashi-			18.4								10.0	
Bangla Congress		ipara)	46.9	48.2							**50.0**	**44.3**	16.0	
CPI					5.7					19.8			6.6	
CPM						34.0							20.0	36.4
Forward Bloc	1.0													
Worker's Party													**26.6**	
RSP					11.3									
PSP	2.9													
Jana Sangh	30.1									1.6				
SUC										5.2				
SBP												1.9		
PML										20.0				
Independents	4.5, 3.4		26.9, 22.8, 0.7	18.4, 6.4				25.9, 10.1, 6.9, 4.6, 4.0, 2.8	13.0, 8.0		8.3, 3.1			7.5, 1.0

NADIA DISTRICT	68. CHAPRA							69. NABADWIP						
	1952	1957	1962	1967	1969	1971	1972	1952	1957	1962	1967	1969	1971	1972
Congress	**56.3**	49.0	30.2	39.8	16.8		**60.4**	**39.9**	50.0	30.0	**50.9**	**51.8**	18.7	**69.3**
Congress (O)					5.6								22.4	3.8
Bangla Congress			**60.2**	**40.5**	17.7								2.1	
CPI								36.6	47.0	**55.6**				
CPM					**41.1**	35.6					44.3	45.9	**56.0**	26.9
PSP	15.0													
Forward Bloc								4.3						
Proutist					0.8							2.3		
Jan Sangh	2.0		1.4							5.0	4.8			
RRP	0.9													
INDF					0.9									
PML					18.1									
Muslim League								4.0						
SBP		**51.0**												
Independents	20.1, 5.7		5.4, 2.8	18.8				15.2, 2.6, 1.4	3.0	9.4			0.8	

Nadia District	70. Krishnagar West							71. Krishnagar East						
	1952	1957	1962	1967	1969	1971	1972	1952	1957	1962	1967	1969	1971	1972
Congress				37.7	40.0	26.6	**63.4**				32.0	37.5		**75.8**
Congress (O)	(See Krishnagar)					2.2		(See Krishnagar)					19.4	
Bangla Congress						3.7								
CPI						11.2								
CPM				**43.6**	**50.7**	**50.8**	36.6						31.8	23.1
SSP				9.1							**68.0**	58.1		
INDF												1.1		
Proutist					1.1							0.9		
PML					4.6									
Independents				7.4	2.3	5.6						1.7	**48.9**	1.1
				2.2	1.3	0.5						0.7		

Nadia District	72. Hanskhali							73. Santipur						
	1952	1957	1962	1967	1969	1971	1972	1952	1957	1962	1967	1969	1971	1972
Congress	**38.6**			32.9	45.7	**45.5**	**68.5**	**38.1**	**46.9**	32.0	38.2	42.2	39.1	**59.4**
Congress (O)						1.8							4.3	
Bangla Congress			**67.1**	**51.8**	8.8									
CPI	33.5				8.1									
CPM						35.8	31.5				**47.6**			
PSP								12.9						
RCPI								21.4	36.8	**54.1**		47.5	39.7	40.6
INDF					2.0							3.2		
Proutist					0.6									
HMS	2.9													
Jana Sangh								12.4						
SBP										13.9				
Independents	25.0							11.9	12.2		9.7	7.2	8.8	
								2.0	4.2		4.5		6.9	
								1.3					1.2	

NADIA DISTRICT	74. RANAGHAT WEST							75. RANAGHAT EAST						
	1952	1957	1962	1967	1969	1971	1972	1952	1957	1962	1967	1969	1971	1972
Congress			**49.6**	40.1	46.6	**60.5**				40.8	43.6	33.0		
Congress (O)					0.9							1.8	1.7	
Bangla Congress											0.7			
CPI										**50.5**	**55.7**	26.9	**65.9**	
CPM			42.5	**53.7**	**49.0**	39.5						**37.6**	32.4	
RSP					2.8									
Lok Dal				3.6										
INDF												0.7		
Proutist				0.6										
Independents			7.9	2.0	0.8					8.8				

NADIA DISTRICT	76. CHAKDAH							77. HARINGHATA						
	1952	1957	1962	1967	1969	1971	1972	1952	1957	1962	1967	1969	1971	1972
Congress (1)	42.7	**51.6**	26.1	28.8		**57.4**		**25.9**	**48.2**	41.0	44.5	44.1		
Congress (2)								**25.3**						
Congress (O)													0.8	1.9
Bangla Congress			42.1	56.1	28.8									
CPI (1)		28.5			7.8			22.0	36.1	16.3				**56.2**
CPI (2)								21.8						
CPM					**50.9**	42.6						**48.6**	42.0	
PSP	**52.2**													
Jana Sangh									0.4					
Forward Bloc														
BBC				13.2								0.9	6.5	
RCPI					9.3									
INDF				0.9										
Lok Dal												1.1		
Proutist				1.0										
Independents	5.1	18.1	30.2		3.3			2.4	9.2	**42.7**	**53.5**			
		2.0	1.6					1.7	5.4					
								1.0	0.6					
								0.1						

NADIA DISTRICT — Others : KRISHNAGAR

	1952	1957	1962	1967	1969	1971	1972
Congress (1)	**53.2**	**62.0**	35.5				
Congress (2)							
CPI				(See Krishnagar East and West)			
CPM							
PSP	9.5		**46.8**				
Jana Sangh							
Forward Bloc			5.0				
HMS							
Independents	16.8	38.0	12.0				
	10.5		0.7				
	7.0						
	3.1						

NADIA DISTRICT — Others : RANAGHAT

	1952	1957	1962	1967	1969	1971	1972
Congress (1)	**30.8**	**41.6**	39.1				
Congress (2)	**25.4**			(See Ranaghat East and Ranaghat West)			
CPI				46.8			
PSP	14.2	32.3	8.6				
Jana Sangh	5.6	6.5					
HMS	7.1						
Independents	7.2	11.8	3.4				
	5.0	5.0	2.1				
	2.9	2.8					
	1.8						

24-PARGANAS DISTRICT — 78. BAGDAHA

	1952	1957	1962	1967	1969	1971	1972
Congress (1)		**45.6**	28.9	39.4			
Congress (2)							
Congress (O)							
Bangla Congress					13.8		
CPI		19.3					
CPM					35.9	36.7	
PSP							
Forward Bloc				**71.1**	**53.1**	**48.9**	
Jana Sangh						1.4	
HMS		2.3					
Proutist							
Republican				**7.5**			
Independents		23.8					**63.3**
		9.0					

24-PARGANAS DISTRICT — 79. BONGAON

	1952	1957	1962	1967	1969	1971	1972
Congress (1)	**37.3**	**22.9**	**56.9**	**35.1**	42.0		
Congress (2)		19.6					
Congress (O)						5.6	
Bangla Congress						11.0	
CPI	34.3	**27.1**	31.0	26.2	**56.4**	**44.9**	**64.7**
CPM					23.9	38.4	35.3
PSP	7.2	13.4	9.0				
Jana Sangh	2.6		1.0				
HMS		4.8	2.0				
Proutist					1.2		
Republican						0.4	
Independents	16.4	10.1		13.3			
	1.4	1.3		1.5			
	1.0	0.9					

24-PARGANAS DISTRICT	80. GAIGHATA							81. ASHOKENAGAR						
	1952	1957	1962	1967	1969	1971	1972	1952	1957	1962	1967	1969	1971	1972
Congress	**56.3**		33.8	39.6		**37.6**	**66.3**			32.0	31.4		32.3	
Congress (O)		(See Bongaon)				4.0		(See Habra)					2.1	0.9
Bangla Congress			**39.2**	**45.8**	0.9									
CPI						25.1				**34.1**	**56.5**		21.9	21.3
CPM						32.4	33.7			28.8			**43.1**	35.2
PSP	5.3									4.0				
Forward Bloc	2.8													
Jana Sangh			0.6	7.9										
Lok Dal				0.5										
Proutist				0.9										
Republican				5.3										
BJD											1.1			
PML											11.1			
Independents	11.2		22.6								1.2		0.6	**42.6**
	9.9		1.9											
	7.2		1.9											
	3.7													
	3.0													
	0.8													

24-PARGANAS DISTRICT	82. BARASAT							83. RAJARHAT						
	1952	1957	1962	1967	1969	1971	1972	1952	1957	1962	1967	1969	1971	1972
Congress	**85.8**	28.0	**50.7**	40.4	34.2		**58.2**	**53.0**	23.1	36.0			**46.9**	**55.4**
Congress (O)						8.1								
Bangla Congress						8.1					24.0		2.0	
CPM						31.8					**30.3**	**44.8**	38.6	44.6
PSP	1.7													
Forward Bloc	10.7	**40.0**	44.1	**58.3**	**46.8**	34.4	40.3						6.6	
Lok Dal												17.2		
INDF					0.2									
BNP					1.5									
Republican							1.5					1.2		
PML					17.1									
Independents	1.8	23.0	5.0	1.3	0.2	16.6		47.0	22.6			0.7	6.0	
		6.3	0.2											
	1.3													
	0.9													
	0.5													

24-Parganas District	84. Deganga							85. Habra						
	1952	1957	1962	1967	1969	1971	1972	1952	1957	1962	1967	1969	1971	1972
Congress (1)	**78.5**	**24.8**	**60.3**	23.3	18.0	21.4	**41.3**	**52.0**	**61.0**	**62.6**	44.3	**47.9**	**52.7**	**66.0**
Congress (2)		20.8												
Congress (O)					1.0	1.1							2.6	
Bangla Congress				**73.1**	30.5	**46.8**					**50.0**	39.5		
CPI		19.9				16.9			35.3	35.8				
CPM													28.2	30.5
PSP (1)								14.3						
PSP (2)								7.5						
SSP											5.7			
Forward Bloc								23.3						
Lok Dal												0.7		
Proutist					3.9							0.2		
INDF					3.1									
HMS									0.9					
Swatantra			4.7											
PML					**44.4**							11.7		
Muslim League							40.6							2.1
SBP										1.0				
Independents	14.5	10.3	32.0	3.6		10.8	17.0	1.9	1.9	0.5			15.0	1.4
Independents	2.7	7.8	3.0			2.4		1.0	0.9				1.6	
Independents	2.4	6.0				0.7								
Independents	2.0	5.5												
Independents		4.1												
Independents		0.8												

24-Parganas District	86. Swarupnagar							87. Baduria						
	1952	1957	1962	1967	1969	1971	1972	1952	1957	1962	1967	1969	1971	1972
Congress	**50.9**	**35.3**	**50.2**	39.1	38.6	**48.9**	**70.8**	**57.5**	**52.6**	37.4	40.9		**50.3**	**64.3**
Congress (O)						1.8	0.9							3.5
Bangla Congress											29.0			0.6
CPI	27.1	34.7	48.98	**56.7**	**47.1**	23.8		30.1	43.5				7.0	
CPM						18.0	28.3				33.6	**55.0**	30.8	35.7
Jana Sangh										3.0				
RRP	1.6													
Lok Dal					7.2								1.1	
INDF					1.0								0.3	
PML					6.1								2.8	
Independents	12.4	19.3		4.2		7.5		8.1	0.9				7.7	
Independents	6.7	8.3						4.3						
Independents	1.3	2.4												

24-PARGANAS DISTRICT	88. BASIRHAT							89. HASNABAD						
	1952	1957	1962	1967	1969	1971	1972	1952	1957	1962	1967	1969	1971	1972
Congress (1)	**43.6**	**39.0**	**59.1**	31.6	44.4	**50.3**	**62.9**	17.4	25.0	61.2	26.8	36.1	**50.5**	**66.4**
Congress (2)								**13.0**	22.0					
Congress (O)						0.2								
Bangla Congress											47.4		3.0	
CPI (1)		35.9	**64.6**	**51.2**	13.8			12.6	**25.0**	35.0		**42.5**	16.2	
CPI (2)								13.0						
CPM				3.8		21.5	37.1				14.4		22.4	33.6
PSP		37.0	5.0						14.0					
Forward Bloc (1)	3.2													
Forward Bloc (2)	1.6													
RCPI								7.4						
Jana Sangh		5.5						4.4	6.0					
HMS								2.6						
Lok Dal					1.7						19.0			
INDF											0.8			
PML					2.6						0.9			
Independents	23.4	17.5			0.2	14.1		10.8	4.5	2.5	11.4	0.9	7.9	
	11.2	1.0						5.5	3.5	1.3				
	15.0							3.6						
	0.6							3.6						
	0.8							2.6						
	0.6							1.7						
								0.8						
								0.7						
								0.7						
								0.5						

24-PARGANAS DISTRICT	90. HINGALGANJ							91. GOSABHA						
	1952	1957	1962	1967	1969	1971	1972	1952	1957	1962	1967	1969	1971	1972
Congress	(See Kalinagar)		24.0	38.6				(See Sandeshkhali)		24.9	40.5	42.0	**53.1**	
Congress (O)					25.0	2.6							1.1	
Bangla Congress												1.1		
CPI				31.0	**54.3**	23.1	**35.7**							
CPM					27.3	34.8						10.2		
RSP											36.4	**59.2**	**43.7**	43.2
INDF					7.1									
Jana Sangh											38.7			
Independents				31.8	22.8	26.9						0.3	1.2	2.6
				13.3	1.1							1.1		
					0.8							0.6		

24-PARGANAS DISTRICT	92. SANDESHKHALI							93. HAROA						
	1952	1957	1962	1967	1969	1971	1972	1952	1957	1962	1967	1969	1971	1972
Congress	25.9	**41.6**	**42.0**	35.9	40.6	**53.1**		46.9	45.8	24.9	33.9		**43.4**	**54.2**
Congress (O)												0.8		
Bangla Congress										61.1	40.7		3.8	
CPI			20.4		9.8			30.3					9.0	
CPM				33.1	**60.6**	**40.7**	46.9						34.3	45.8
RSP	**36.7**	32.4			6.4									
Jana Sangh	4.6	22.0							1.2	4.0				
Lok Dal												21.3		
INDF												1.2		
PML												3.0		
Independents	6.5	4.0	4.5	3.5	2.6			11.1	40.6	11.5			8.6	
	6.3							6.8	8.2	2.6				
	5.0							3.7	1.4					
	3.9													
	3.5													
	3.1													
	2.7													
	1.8													

24-PARGANAS DISTRICT	94. BASANTI							95. CANNING						
	1952	1957	1962	1967	1969	1971	1972	1952	1957	1962	1967	1969	1971	1972
Congress (1)			**60.3**	**38.5**	35.6	**31.5**	50.8	30.5	**48.8**	41.8	**48.1**	37.0		57.3
Congress (2)	(See							28.6						
Bangla Congress	Canning)		8.6							58.2	25.6	3.3		
CPI (1)								20.4						
CPI (2)								14.9						
CPM					25.4								36.7	41.8
RSP			8.8	35.9	**39.0**	22.0	44.7		1.8					
SUC			8.6						1.6				22.1	
Lok Dal				2.6										
INDF												3.4		
Proutist												7.3		
Jana Sangh														0.9
PML				8.3								0.8		
Muslim League						4.5								
Independents			18.4	12.7	14.5	17.1		5.6	47.8			12.3	1.0	
			3.6	3.3		3.9						2.3		
			0.3	0.9										

24-Parganas District	96. KULTALI							97. JOYNAGAR						
	1952	1957	1962	1967	1969	1971	1972	1952	1957	1962	1967	1969	1971	1972
Congress (1)	(See Joynagar South)			38.0	46.0	42.0	**54.8**	11.4	13.5	(See Joynagar North)	25.4	44.0	40.8	**51.6**
Congress (2)								9.6	11.5					
Congress (O)						0.6								
Bangla Congress						0.4								
CPM						12.8							6.2	
SUC				**60.5**	**52.4**	**44.2**	45.2	**15.6**	**20.0**		**61.6**	**54.9**	**41.2**	48.4
Lok Dal					1.3									
INDF					0.3									
Jana Sangh (1)								12.8						
Jana Sangh (2)								6.4						
PML													0.9	
RRP								1.3						
Independents				1.5				**13.5**	**14.5**		10.5		11.9	
								11.3	13.0		1.4			
								5.1	13.1		1.1			
								4.7	4.2					
								3.3	3.6					
								2.6	3.5					
								2.4	3.4					

24-Parganas District	98. BARUIPUR							99. SONARPUR						
	1952	1957	1962	1967	1969	1971	1972	1952	1957	1962	1967	1969	1971	1972
Congress (1)	13.8	16.1	**57.2**	25.6	43.2	35.3	**55.2**			27.0	32.0	42.6	19.6	
Congress (2)	**16.1**	15.8						(See Baruipur)						
Congress (O)													0.8	
Bangla Congress				32.5		1.6								
CPI (1)	15.5	**26.9**	32.5							**52.0**	8.8		25.4	**56.1**
CPI (2)		**25.9**												
CPM						**36.1**	41.3				36.1	**56.8**	**54.3**	42.7
PSP			6.4							7.0				
SSP				**42.0**	**50.9**	11.3								
Proutist					1.6									
INDF												0.8		
Jana Sangh (1)	3.6						0.6							
Jana Sangh (2)	3.5													
MuslimLeague							2.9							
Independents	9.3	5.4	3.9		4.4	15.7				14.0	15.4			0.8
	7.1	3.6									7.1			0.3
	7.0	2.8									0.5			
	5.6	1.9												
	4.7	1.8												
	3.7													
	3.6													
	2.7													
	2.1													
	1.0													
	0.8													

24-PARGANAS DISTRICT

	100. BHANGAR							101. JADAVPUR						
	1952	1957	1962	1967	1969	1971	1972	1952	1957	1962	1967	1969	1971	1972
Congress (1)	12.6	**43.9**	**57.6**	23.3	**34.7**	16.6	28.9			43.6	34.5			42.6
Congress (2)	**17.8**													
Congress (O)					9.8			(See					5.5	
Bangla Congress				76.7	23.8	1.9		Sonarpur)						
CPI (1)	**17.0**	27.7	14.9		23.5								29.0	
CPI (2)	16.2													
CPM						23.5	**33.6**			50.9	**63.3**	**57.6**	**55.7**	
PSP			3.3							1.8				
RSP													7.2	
Jana Sangh (1)	4.4													
Jana Sangh (2)	4.1													
Swatantra			2.0											
INDF				0.7										
Lok Dal				28.4										
Proutist												2.2		
PML				3.4										
Muslim League						27.3								
Independents	13.0	28.5	22.0		9.0	24.6	9.3			1.9			0.7	0.9
	6.3		0.2			0.9				1.9				0.8
	4.7													
	2.2													
	1.9													

24-PARGANAS DISTRICT

	102. BEHALA EAST							103. BEHALA WEST						
	1952	1957	1962	1967	1969	1971	1972	1952	1957	1962	1967	1969	1971	1972
Congress				34.7	34.8	43.3	**60.7**					44.1	33.1	
Congress (O)	(See Behala)					4.3		(See Behala)					6.0	
CPI				19.0									43.1	**51.5**
CPM				**45.8**	**63.0**	52.4	39.3				**55.9**	**57.0**	**51.0**	48.5
Jana Sangh					2.3									
Lok Dal													0.7	
Republican													1.5	
PML													7.7	
Independents				0.6										

24-PARGANAS DISTRICT	104. GARDEN REACH							105. MAHESHTOLA						
	1952	1957	1962	1967	1969	1971	1972	1952	1957	1962	1967	1969	1971	1972
Congress	**50.0**	39.4	**59.0**	**38.9**	17.7	**34.2**	47.7	**24.6**	35.0	**57.7**	36.8	30.3	42.2	**56.6**
CPI	31.3	**51.6**	41.0		**57.5**	27.7		**25.3**	**41.4**	33.5	9.7			
CPM						34.0	**50.4**				**53.5**	**47.2**	**44.8**	43.4
PSP	2.8							3.2		4.6				
Forward Bloc	1.2													
Worker's Party										4.2				
Jana Sangh	8.6													
HMS		1.9												
Lok Dal					19.2									
INDF					0.2									
PML					4.6							22.5		
Independents	5.2	6.2		28.5	0.6	3.1	1.9	23.2	14.0				13.0	
	0.6	1.0		15.5	0.1	1.1		12.7	9.7					
	0.3			13.4				6.8						
				2.8				4.2						
				0.9										

24-PARGANAS DISTRICT	106. BUDGE BUDGE							107. BISHNUPUR WEST						
	1952	1957	1962	1967	1969	1971	1972	1952	1957	1962	1967	1969	1971	1972
Congress	24.0	35.5	**48.8**	35.7	38.9					**52.5**	42.4	41.8	34.6	48.2
Congress (O)						2.4		(See					1.8	2.5
Bangla Congress						2.8		Bishnu-					0.9	
CPI	**49.9**	**51.5**	45.0			29.2	38.4	pur)		43.5				
CPM				**53.7**	**61.1**	**60.6**	**61.6**				**56.7**	**53.6**	**58.7**	**49.3**
PSP			5.0											
Forward Bloc				6.8									2.1	
Worker's Party			0.4											
RCPI	4.5													
Lok Dal												1.0		
INDF												0.6		
Proutist												0.6		
PML												2.3		
Independents	9.2	13.0	0.5	3.7		5.0				2.6	0.9		1.9	
	5.6		0.3							1.4				
	4.0													
	1.4													
	0.8													
	0.7													

24-PARGANAS DISTRICT	108. BISHNUPUR EAST							109. FALTA						
	1952	1957	1962	1967	1969	1971	1972	1952	1957	1962	1967	1969	1971	1972
Congress			**61.1**	26.0	44.6	**46.6**	**58.6**	25.1	**52.0**	**52.7**	33.8	42.5	28.7	**53.7**
Congress (O)	(See				1.2								3.8	
Bangla Congress	Bishnu-												0.8	
CPI	pur)		23.4	9.4				**37.2**	48.0	39.1				
CPM				**39.7**	**48.9**	45.0	41.4				**54.0**	**57.5**	**57.5**	45.4
PSP								23.7						
SSP						1.2								
Jana Sangh								10.3						
Lok Dal					1.6									
PML					5.0									
Independents			7.2	18.4		6.0		3.8		4.1	6.5		9.1	0.9
			6.5	5.3						3.9	4.8			
			1.8	1.2						0.5	1.0			
										0.3				
										0.3				
										0.1				

24-PARGANAS DISTRICT	110. DIAMOND HARBOUR							111. MAGRAHAT EAST						
	1952	1957	1962	1967	1969	1971	1972	1952	1957	1962	1967	1969	1971	1972
Congress	21.8	28.0	**40.5**	25.7	38.2	46.0	**56.9**		*	44.7	48.0		37.0	**56.9**
Congress (O)						2.0		(See					1.0	
Bangla Congress				34.6				Magrahat)						
CPI			21.3											
CPM				**38.3**	**56.7**	**50.9**	43.1			**51.4**	**51.2**		**39.8**	42.7
PSP	**44.7**	**39.0**	13.0											
Jana Sangh				1.4								1.2		
SUC													5.6	
Forward Bloc						1.2								
Independents	20.5	28.0	25.2		2.7					2.8	0.8		16.6	0.5
	7.8	5.0			2.5									
	2.8													
	2.5													

*Won unopposed

24-Parganas District	112. MAGRAHAT WEST							113. KULPI						
	1952	1957	1962	1967	1969	1971	1972	1952	1957	1962	1967	1969	1971	1972
Congress (1)			**52.1**	32.7	25.9	19.2	**51.7**	9.6	53.0	43.5	**53.6**	45.6		**64.8**
Congress (2)								9.6						
Congress (O)	(See					4.1	2.5						20.3	2.5
Bangla Congress	Magrahat)			**47.4**	**34.1**	33.5					46.4	**50.5**	20.2	
CPI			33.4											
CPM				19.3		33.2	45.9						**24.4**	
PSP (1)					1.4			**22.0**	38.0					
PSP (2)								13.4						
SUC						3.1				5.9			17.7	32.4
Jana Sangh (1)				0.6				**15.2**						
Jana Sangh (2)								9.5						
Lok Dal					26.3									
Independents			7.8		12.2	6.8		11.5	9.0	**46.8**		3.9	15.8	0.3
			3.4					4.8		1.5			1.6	
			3.3					4.5		1.5				
										0.8				

24-Parganas District	114. MATHARAPUR							115. PATHARPRATIMA						
	1952	1957	1962	1967	1969	1971	1972	1952	1957	1962	1967	1969	1971	1972
Congress (1)	**10.0**	**24.5**		32.5	48.3	30.6	**57.9**				30.4	39.0	14.9	**49.5**
Congress (2)	8.6	**25.5**												
Congress (O)						2.7		(See						
Bangla Congress				**34.6**		9.3		Mathurapur			30.0		14.6		
CPI	6.6							and						
CPM						5.1		Mathurapur SE)					17.0		
PSP (1)	**15.4**	13.5	(See Mathurapur SE)											
PSP (2)	5.7	12.0												
SUC	11.5	8.2		33.0	**50.9**	**41.8**	41.9				**36.5**	**57.0**	**41.1**	48.6
RCPI												0.4		
Jan Sangh (1)	7.2													
Jan Sangh (2)	6.8													
INDF					0.7							3.3		
Independents	8.8	7.8				9.3	1.8				2.0	0.3	10.1	1.9
	7.8	4.0				1.2	0.2				0.8		2.4	
	7.2	2.9												
	4.3	1.6												

24-PARGANAS DISTRICT	116. KAKDWIP							117. SAGAR						
	1952	1957	1962	1967	1969	1971	1972	1952	1957	1962	1967	1969	1971	1972
Congress		**64.0**	**34.3**	**73.6**	**49.8**	14.9	**59.5**	26.6			**37.4**	39.6	26.7	
Congress (O)					18.5			(See					6.3	
Bangla Congress					11.5			Kakdwip)			**60.4**	12.6	3.7	
CPI			22.9		10.3		19.7			28.2			20.6	
CPM				23.3	44.4	**44.6**	40.5					**41.3**	**42.7**	
PSP	36.0	14.6					**35.2**							
Jana Sangh			2.4				6.4			0.9				
INDF				2.1										
Lok Dal				3.8										
Independents			28.2	0.8			8.5			31.5		9.4	33.0	
							2.7			2.0		3.7		
							1.0							

24-PARGANAS DISTRICT	118. BIJPUR							119. NAIHATI						
	1952	1957	1962	1967	1969	1971	1972	1952	1957	1962	1967	1969	1971	1972
Congress	**49.5**	41.8	43.5	35.8	48.0	**51.1**	**61.2**	**50.1**	40.4	47.0	**46.8**	43.2		**52.5**
Congress (O)													3.7	
Bangla Congress													1.0	
CPI	35.8	**50.3**	47.2	18.6				37.2	**52.4**	**51.2**	13.1			
CPM				**38.7**	51.4	48.9	38.8				39.6	**55.6**	**54.4**	46.9
PSP	3.2		8.0											
SSP													1.3	
Forward Bloc	5.7							6.2						
Bolshevik Party								1.1						
Jana Sangh				1.8				5.4			0.5			
HMS		2.9												
Swatantra										1.8				
Proutist												0.5		
Republican												0.7		
Independents	3.9	3.2	1.0	4.4	0.4			4.0					38.2	0.6
	1.9	0.9	0.3	0.6	0.2			1.7					0.8	
		0.9						1.5					0.6	

24-PARGANAS DISTRICT	120. BHATPARA							121. NOAPARA						
	1952	1957	1962	1967	1969	1971	1972	1952	1957	1962	1967	1969	1971	1972
Congress	**74.7**	39.0	**55.4**	**49.5**	46.5	**49.9**	**57.7**	40.0	44.3	**42.6**	42.7	25.4		**67.3**
Congress (O)						1.3							1.5	
CPI		**39.9**	42.8	2.0						**48.0**				
CPM				42.1	**49.8**	46.7	41.8				42.6	**55.0**	**53.4**	31.6
PSP	2.0			0.7				**58.6**	7.0					
Forward Bloc					2.1								19.7	
Bolshevik Party	10.5													
Jana Sangh	10.0					0.5					2.7	1.7		0.4
RRP	1.5													
INDF					0.5									
Proutist												0.6		
Lok Dal					2.1									
Swatantra										0.7				
Republican					1.1									
Independents	0.7	12.0	1.2	2.9					1.4	12.1				0.7
	0.7	6.9	0.6	1.9										
		1.3		1.0										
		0.9												

24-PARGANAS DISTRICT	122. TITAGARH							123. KHARDAH						
	1952	1957	1962	1967	1969	1971	1972	1952	1957	1962	1967	1969	1971	1972
Congress	**50.9**	**44.3**	**50.1**	**36.6**	42.3	44.9	**68.6**	33.3	31.3	31.8	41.7			
Congress (O)						1.5							1.7	
CPI			46.0	24.5						**58.1**	31.6		46.1	**74.1**
CPM				35.0	**57.3**	**53.6**	31.4				**34.8**	**57.3**	**52.1**	25.9
PSP	6.3							**64.3**	10.4					
Forward Bloc		35.8												
Bolshevik Party	9.7													
Jana Sangh	15.4	3.4		3.1							1.7			
Swatantra			3.2											
INDF					0.4								0.9	
Independents	8.7	9.4	0.7	0.8				2.4	0.2					
	4.1	7.1												
	3.2													
	1.7													

24-Parganas District	124. PANIHATA							125. KAMARHATI						
	1952	1957	1962	1967	1969	1971	1972	1952	1957	1962	1967	1969	1971	1972
Congress				32.8	28.8		**72.7**				36.8	34.1		**55.4**
Congress (O)	(See Khardah)					5.6							6.1	
Bangla Congress										9.4				
CPI				15.0		27.7							26.1	
CPM				**47.7**	**69.7**	**66.7**	26.8				**51.3**	**65.1**	**67.7**	43.5
PSP				3.8										
Jana Sangh				0.8						1.3				
INDF					1.5							0.8		
Republican							0.5							
Independents											1.2			1.2

24-Parganas District	126. BARANAGAR							127. DUM DUM						
	1952	1957	1962	1967	1969	1971	1972	1952	1957	1962	1967	1969	1971	1972
Congress	34.4	39.5	38.1	46.7	37.8			**30.5**	33.0	37.4	44.4	40.6		**85.7**
Bangla Congress					42.7									
CPI	**56.2**	**59.2**	**56.9**			**69.6**		3.9		**58.8**				
CPM				**52.5**	**61.8**	**57.3**	30.4				**53.6**	**59.4**	**56.0**	14.1
PSP	1.7		1.3					7.4	**58.5**	3.8				
Forward Bloc								14.0						
RSP	0.3							2.4						
Jana Sangh			2.0					0.9	2.5					
Swatantra			0.7											
HMS			0.9											
Proutist														
Independents	6.1	0.9	0.1	0.8	0.5			20.1	5.5		2.0		43.2	0.2
	1.0	0.4						17.7	0.5				0.8	
	0.3							0.6						
								0.5						
								2.1						

24-Parganas District — Others: BISHNUPUR

	1952	1957	1962	1967	1969	1971	1972
Congress (1)	**14.8**	20.2					
Congress (2)	18.5	18.9					
CPI (1)	**24.3**	21.7					
CPI (2)		**21.7**					
PSP (1)	2.2						
PSP (2)	3.2						
Forward Bloc							
RCPI (1)	4.3						
RCPI (2)	3.9						
Jana Sangh (1)	8.1						
Jana Sangh (2)	6.7						
Independents	7.8	6.3					
	2.7	2.9					
	1.6	2.6					
	1.1	2.4					
	0.8	2.2					
		1.2					

(See Bishnupur East and West)

24-Parganas District — Others: BEHALA

	1952	1957	1962	1967	1969	1971	1972
Congress (1)	26.1	33.3	38.0				
CPI (1)		**64.8**	54.8				
PSP (1)	2.4						
Forward Bloc	**41.7**						
Jana Sangh (1)	3.3						
Independents	20.0	1.1	7.2				
	4.3	0.8					
	1.3						
	0.9						

(See Behala East and West)

24-Parganas District — Others: KALINAGAR

	1952	1957	1962	1967	1969	1971	1972
Congress	**55.0**						
CPI	41.0						
Forward Bloc							
RSP							
Jana Sangh							
Independents	4.0						

(See Hingalganj)

24-Parganas District — Others: BARRACKPUR

	1952	1957	1962	1967	1969	1971	1972
Congress	**41.9**						
CPI							
Forward Bloc	28.9						
RSP	14.1						
Jana Sangh	14.1						
Independents	1.1						

24-Parganas District — Others: JOYNAGAR NORTH

	1952	1957	1962	1967	1969	1971	1972
Congress	**52.2**						
SUC	43.8						
Independents	4.0						

(See Joynagar)

24-Parganas District — Others: JOYNAGAR SOUTH

	1952	1957	1962	1967	1969	1971	1972
Congress	**59.9**						
SUC	33.9						
Independents	6.2						

(See Kutali)

24-PARGANAS DISTRICT	*Others :* MAGRAHAT							*Others-:* MATHURAPUR (NW)						
	1952	1957	1962	1967	1969	1971	1972	1952	1957	1962	1967	1969	1971	1972
Congress (1)	**21.4**	**29.0**						**52.3**						
Congress (2)	**23.2**	**26.0**	(See							(See				
CPI		16.0	Magrahat East							Mathurapur)				
PSP (1)	4.7	12.0	and					31.8						
PSP (2)	3.1		Magrahat West)											
SUC								14.1						
Jana Sangh (1)	7.7													
Jana Sangh (2)	6.4													
Independents	10.6	10.0						1.8						
	6.1	4.2												
	5.1	2.8												
	5.0													
	3.2													
	2.1													
	1.8													

24-PARGANAS DISTRICT	*Others :* MATHURAPUR (SE)							*Others :* HAROA-SANDESHKHALI						
	1952	1957	1962	1967	1969	1971	1972	1952	1957	1962	1967	1969	1971	1972
Congress (1)			**45.2**					11.7						
Congress (2)			(See					12.9		(See				
CPI			30.9	Mathurapur)				**20.1**		Sandeshkhali)				
SUC			16.9											
RSP								11.0						
Bolshevik Party								5.7						
Swatantra			7.0											
Independents								10.8						
								7.2						
								5.5						
								5.4						
								4.2						
								2.7						
								1.5						
								1.4						

24-PARGANAS DISTRICT	*Others :* TOLLYGANJ						
	1952	1957	1962	1967	1969	1971	1972
Congress	24.5						
PSP (1)	6.4						
PSP (2)	1.6						
RSP	6.4						
Jana Sangh	5.3						
Independents	**37.4**						
	7.1						
	6.8						
	1.9						
	1.0						
	0.6						
	0.5						
	0.5						
	0.1						

CALCUTTA	128. COSSIPUR							129. SHAMPUKUR						
	1952	1957	1962	1967	1969	1971	1972	1952	1957	1962	1967	1969	1971	1972
Congress	**45.2**	47-2	**46.4**	**36.1**	49.4	**59.7**	71.8	26.1	26.9	31.2	**47.8**	45.1		**66.2**
Congress (O)					1.2									
CPI	39.3		45.6					2.7						
CPM				30.6	**49.8**	36.4	28.2				45.9		(Election Not Held)	31.9
PSP	5.0	**50.6**	7.3											
Forward Bloc				14.6				9.9	**73.1**	**67.6**		**54.5**		
Jana Sangh			0.8	5.2		2.7					6.4			
HMS	4.5							2.4						
Independents	3.4	2.2		13.5	0.8			**58.1**		1.2		0.4		1.5
	2.1							0.9						0.4
	0.5													

CALCUTTA	130. JORABAGAN							131. JORASANKO						
	1951	1957	1962	1967	1969	1971	1972	1952	1957	1962	1967	1969	1971	1972
Congress	**42.6**	**46.7**	**59.1**	38.8	**50.5**	**65.8**	**76.5**	31.3	**59.8**	**57.1**	**46.4**	**44.7**	**49.2**	**71.8**
Bangla Congress					2.5									
CPI	32.2													
CPM				**43.4**	48.7	31.7	23.5						23.0	27.8
PSP	2.4		0.4					1.0		0.5				
Forward Bloc		40.3	33.3					**62.6**	37.7	38.0	5.9	35.2	4.2	
Jana Sangh			3.1	6.2	17.7				3.0	42.1	19.7	22.7		
INDF												0.1		
Proutist				0.5										
Independents	16.3	9.2	0.6	0.3				1.9	2.5	0.5	3.8	0.3	0.3	0.4
	3.3	0.7	0.4					1.6		0.3	0.7		0.3	
	1.3							1.5		0.3	0.6		0.2	
	1.2									0.2	0.5		0.1	
	0.7													

CALCUTTA	132. BARABAZAR							133. BOWBAZAR						
	1952	1957	1962	1967	1969	1971	1972	1952	1957	1962	1967	1969	1971	1972
Congress	**71.5**	**74.8**	**74.4**	**54.5**	**55.5**	**55.6**	**76.7**	**58.7**	**50.1**	**61.8**	**57.5**	**56.0**	**60.7**	**64.6**
CPI			14.5					48.3	36.1					
CPM						15.0	21.3				14.2		30.4	35.4
PSP	3.3		0.9		0.3					0.4				
SSP				4.9	16.9	0.3								
Forward Bloc	16.2						41.3				19.8	35.3	2.8	
RSP					0.5	0.6								
Jan Sangh		8.6		37.0	25.1	28.3					8.1	7.9	6.1	
HMS										1.6				
Swatantra														
RRP	5.3									1.7				
Independents	1.2	15.4	9.6	1.8	0.9	0.3	1.4				0.5	0.8		
	0.8	1.2	0.6	1.1	0.8									
	0.8			0.4	0.4									
	0.5			0.3	0.1									
	0.5													

CALCUTTA	134. CHOWRINGEE							135. KABITIRTHA						
	1952	1957	1962	1967	1969	1971	1972	1952	1957	1962	1967	1969	1971	1972
Congress		**69.6**	**72.1**	**62.3**	**57.8**	**54.1**	**70.6**	(See		**46.1**	38.7	**42.6**	**50.3**	
Congress (O)						14.1		Fort					1.6	
CPI			23.6					and						
CPM				31.6		26.0	29.4	Ekbalpore)	16.5			26.5		
PSP	27.2										0.3			
Forward Bloc						5.8			35.2	**58.6**	28.5	48.8		
Jana Sangh			0.9	6.1										
Swatantra			1.0											
Republican					42.2						2.0			
Independents		3.2	2.4						0.3	0.2	0.7	0.6		
									2.0	0.2		0.3		

CALCUTTA	136. ALIPORE							137. KALIGHAT						
	1952	1957	1962	1967	1969	1971	1972	1952	1957	1962	1967	1969	1971	1972
Congress	**55.8**	37.0	41.7	48.0	49.2	**46.9**	**68.8**	36.8	48.0	**51.3**	**47.3**	44.8	**55.2**	65.0
Congress (O)						2.6	2.2						5.6	
CPI		**62.0**	**58.3**	**48.5**	**50.5**	35.3		**43.0**	**51.0**	46.6				
CPM							29.1				46.0	**55.2**	35.8	33.7
PSP	4.8							2.1						
SSP													2.9	
RSP								2.3						
INDF					0.1									
Jana Sangh	3.4							9.8			2.9			
HMS														1.0
RRP								1.8						
Independents	32.3	1.0		3.6	0.2	14.8		12.4	1.0	2.1	1.3		0.5	0.3
	2.0					0.3		0.7			1.1			
	1.0							0.6			1.0			
	0.4							0.3			0.4			
	0.4							0.2						

CALCUTTA	138. RASHBEHARI AVENUE							139. TOLLYGUNGE						
	1952	1957	1962	1967	1969	1971	1972	1952	1957	1962	1967	1969	1971	1972
Congress	39.3	38.5	30.4	44.9	**63.4**	**73.4**		29.9	39.9	44.1	35.3			**63.4**
Bangla Congress													7.2	
CPI										**56.2**			33.7	
CPM					31.2	26.6					**53.4**	**63.0**	**59.0**	36.6
PSP	**39.6**	16.2	25.2					**56.5**						
Worker's Party											3.0			
SUC					5.4									
Jana Sangh												2.4	1.3	
HMS											0.9			
Independents	16.4	**45.3**	**44.4**	**56.0**				8.6					0.3	
	4.7							5.0					0.1	

CALCUTTA	140. DHAKURIA							141. BALLYGUNGE						
	1952	1957	1962	1967	1969	1971	1972	1952	1957	1962	1967	1969	1971	1972
Congress			29.7	38.2				43.9	**48.8**	43.0	43.6	**48.6**		**64.1**
Congress (O)	(See Bhowanipur)				8.0								1.2	
CPI			**38.1**	**61.8**	54.4	61.4		**50.1**	48.0					
CPM			32.2			37.5								
Worker's Party										**53.7**	**56.0**	38.4	35.5	
RSP					38.6								9.8	
SUC													1.9	
Jana Sangh									2.2					
INDF												0.5		
SBP									1.0					
Independents								4.5		1.5				0.4
								1.5		1.2				
										0.6				

CALCUTTA	142. BELIAGHATA SOUTH							143. ENTALLY						
	1952	1957	1962	1967	1969	1971	1972	1952	1957	1962	1967	1969	1971	1972
Congress		**46.2**	**56.1**	47.1	**49.1**	**77.2**	**44.4**	37.8	41.9	32.5	32.7			
Congress (O)												12.5		
CPI		46.0				6.6		36.9	**59.5**	**44.1**	**59.5**	**58.5**	35.7	**57.4**
CPM			43.9	**50.7**	44.2		22.8						**44.6**	42.6
PSP		2.7						4.2						
Forward Bloc								1.5						
Jana Sangh					1.4									
HMS								2.5		0.7				
Lok Dal					0.5									
INDF					0.3							8.8		
Independents		5.1						7.3	2.7	12.2	5.6		7.2	
								3.2		0.7	1.8			
										0.4	0.6			

CALCUTTA	144. TALTOLA							145. SEALDAH						
	1952	1957	1962	1967	1969	1971	1972	1952	1957	1962	1967	1969	1971	1972
Congress	**60.4**	46.6	**54.4**	**39.7**	38.5	**48.8**	**54.2**	35.9			**42.5**	44.7	**54.0**	**69.7**
Congress (O)													3.8	
Bangla Congress											23.0			
CPI	26.2	**52.2**	45.4										8.7	
CPM				33.7	**59.9**	44.3	45.4				33.4		28.4	
PSP	4.3			12.4				10.4						
Forward Bloc														30.3
RSP								26.3				**55.3**	5.0	
Jana Sangh	5.8							3.7						
HMS								2.9						
Proutist					1.0									
Independents	2.7	1.2	0.2	7.7	0.6	4.2	0.4	7.5			1.1			
	0.6			2.7		2.7		6.8						
				2.1				4.5						
				0.7				1.1						
				0.5				0.9						
				0.4										

145. SEALDAH, 1957 & 1962: (See Sukeas Street and Muchipara)

CALCUTTA	146. VIDYASAGAR							147. BELIAGATA NORTH						
	1952	1957	1962	1967	1969	1971	1972	1952	1957	1962	1967	1969	1971	1972
Congress	27.1	44.7	45.9	41.0	39.0	**50.2**	**62.1**	40.	34.8	32.9				**78.4**
Congress (O)						2.9								
Bangla Congress						1.7								
CPI		**55.3**	**54.1**			9.7		56.5						
CPM				**56.3**	**59.9**	35.5	37.9			**42.6**	**66.1**	**53.4**	21.6	
Forward Bloc										22.6		46.6		
Worker's Party								20						
Jana Sangh								12						
HMS	3.0													
Independents	**57.2**			2.7	1.1							1.0		
	3.3													
	2.3													
	1.9													
	1.2													
	1.1													
	0.8													
	0.6													
	0.6													
	0.5													
	0.5													

CALCUTTA	148. MANICKTOLA							149. BURTOLA						
	1952	1957	1964	1967	1969	1971	1972	1952	1957	1962	1967	1969	1971	1972
Congress	24.4	30.6	25.0	43.6	39.9	37.0	**29.6**				45.4	44.7	**53.5**	**68.5**
Congress (O)						1.6	1.4						5.6	3.1
CPI	**47.9**	**67.0**	**46.0**	**56.4**	**58.7**	21.8	**65.2**							
CPM						**39.6**	32.6						27.1	28.4
PSP	7.4						29.2							
Forward Bloc	0.9						21.7							
Proutist				1.4										
RSP	3.5										**54.6**	**55.3**	9.8	
Jana Sangh							0.7							
HMS	3.2													
RRP	0.4						0.5							
Independents	7.3	1.6	29.0				11.9						3.2	
	2.4	0.8					4.0						0.7	
	1.0						1.2							
	0.9						1.1							
	0.8						0.8							

(See Burtola North and South)

CALCUTTA	150. BELGACHIA							Others : WATGUNGE						
	1952	1957	1962	1967	1969	1971	1972	1952	1957	1962	1967	1969	1971	1972
Congress	24.9	31.6	46.0	46.2	38.4	47.1	**59.8**	**65.6**						
CPI	**43.9**	**52.3**	**54.0**											
CPM				**50.1**	**61.6**	**52.9**	40.2							
PSP	5.8							5.4						
RSP	2.6													
Bolshevik Party								25.2						
Jana Sangh	2.6													
Independents	8.4	16.1	1.6					1.7						
	3.6		1.1					1.2						
	3.1		1.0					0.9						
	1.9													
	1.6													
	1.1													
	0.2													
	0.2													

CALCUTTA	Others : BURTOLA NORTH							Others : BURTOLA SOUTH						
	1952	1957	1962	1967	1969	1971	1972	1952	1957	1962	1967	1969	1971	1972
Congress	35.8	41.6						37.3	46.2					
CPI			(See							**53.8**	(See			
PSP	**64.2**				Burtola)							Burtola)		
PSP		**55.1**												
Jana Sangh									7.6					
HMS		2.2												
Independents		1.1						**46.6**						
								8.5						

CALCUTTA	*Others :* EKBALPORE							*Others :* FORT						
	1952	1957	1962	1967	1969	1971	1972	1952	1957	1962	1967	1969	1971	1972
Congress	**48.0**	**48.8**						**65.6**	**52.0**	**51.5**				
CPI	27.0		(See								43.5	(See		
PSP			24.2		Kabitirtha)			2.7	23.0				Kabitirtha)	
Jana Sangh								7.1						
Independents	14.0	24.4						14.5	16.0	5.0				
	10.0	2.6						6.1	9.0					
	1.0							2.2						
								1.2						
								0.7						

CALCUTTA	*Others :* COLOOTALA							*Others :* SUKEAS STREET						
	1952	1957	1962	1967	1969	1971	1972	1952	1957	1962	1967	1969	1971	1972
Congress	**70.6**							43.4	**50.9**					
CPI										48.0	(See			
PSP	11.3											Sealdah)		
Bolshevik Party	14.3													
Swatantra									0.4					
Independents	3.8							**53.8**	0.5					
								2.8	0.3					

CALCUTTA	Others : TOLLYGUNGE NORTH							Others : TOLLYGUNGE SOUTH						
	1952	1957	1962	1967	1969	1971	1972	1952	1957	1962	1967	1969	1971	1972
Congress	**27.0**							24.9						
CPI		(See						**44.2**	(See					
PSP	24.3			Tollygunge)				8.7			Tollygunge)			
Forward Bloc	19.4							1.3						
Bolshevik Party	18.0													
Jana Sangh	7.7							13.3						
RRP								0.7						
Independents	2.0							2.6						
	1.3							1.0						
	0.3							0.8						
								0.8						
								0.8						
								0.5						
								0.5						
								0.2						

CALCUTTA	Others : BHAWANIPUR							Others : BELIAGHATA						
	1952	1957	1962	1967	1969	1971	1972	1952	1957	1962	1967	1969	1971	1972
Congress (1)	**37.1**	**50.8**	46.4						18.9					
Congress (2)				(See Tollygunge)					15.8					
CPI (1)									**27.6**					
CPI (2)									**30.4**					
PSP (1)		25.7						22.1						
PSP (2)								3.0						
Forward Bloc									**25.2**					
RSP	13.1													
Jana Sangh	9.5													
RRP	1.3													
Independents	33.1	15.8	**53.6**					23.8	5.2					
	3.1	6.9						10.2	2.1					
	1.4	0.8						6.9						
	1.3							4.1						
								1.8						
								1.4						
								1.0						
								0.5						

CALCUTTA	*Others :* MUCHIPARA							*Others :* BANIAPUKUR-BALLYGUNGE						
	1952	1957	1962	1967	1969	1971	1972	1952	1957	1962	1967	1969	1971	1972
Congress (1)	**33.3**	48.6	**50.8**					**24.5**						
Congress (2)								**19.1**		(See Ballygunge)				
PSP (1)	1.7							2.0						
PSP (2)	0.3							0.9						
Forward Bloc (1)	33.2							7.9						
Forward Bloc (2)								5.5						
RSP		2.2	**50.3**	49.2										
Jana Sangh								7.0						
HMS	9.3													
Independents	10.1	1.1						10.1						
	3.3							8.2						
	2.1							6.0						
	1.7							4.0						
	1.1							2.8						
	0.9							1.2						
	0.4							0.9						
	0.3													
	0.3													
	0.2													

CALCUTTA	*Others :* KUMARTALI						
	1952	1957	1962	1967	1969	1971	1972
Congress	27.3						
PSP	9.3						
Forward Bloc	**33.0**						
Jana Sangh	5.7						
Independents	21.6						
	0.8						
	0.8						
	0.6						
	0.4						
	0.4						

HOWRAH DISTRICT	151. BALLY							152. HOWRAH NORTH						
	1952	1957	1962	1967	1969	1971	1972	1952	1957	1962	1967	1969	1971	1972
Congress	**42.0**	**48.8**	**50.4**	**43.8**	45.1	40.3	**56.2**	31.0	46.8	**61.0**	**51.8**	**49.5**	**53.0**	**59.2**
Congress (O)						5.7								
Bangla Congress				13.1		1.7								
CPI	4.1	47.1	46.5					**51.0**	**47.3**	37.3				
CPM				40.1	**53.4**	**51.3**	43.8					49.0	42.6	40.8
PSP	1.9				0.4			3.1						
Forward Bloc	29.5												1.9	
Jana Sangh	4.9		3.1					3.5			1.2			
RRP	0.7													
Swatantra										0.7				
INDF				0.2								0.8		
Proutist					1.3							0.8		
SSP						0.6								
Independents	8.7	2.9		3.1				6.1	5.9	0.8	38.3		1.3	
	6.9	1.2						2.3		0.2	6.6		1.1	
	0.7							1.8			2.1			
	0.6							1.2						

HOWRAH DISTRICT	153. HOWRAH CENTRAL							154. HOWRAH SOUTH						
	1952	1957	1962	1967	1969	1971	1972	1952	1957	1962	1967	1969	1971	1972
Congress			**41.0**	40.1			**60.3**	**38.0**	39.8	42.1	**54.1**	43.1	**45.7**	**57.0**
Congress (O)	(See Howrah East)				32.8		1.9						3.2	1.9
Bangla Congress					18.8									
CPI								26.4			10.2		12.9	
CPM											34.3	**56.2**	38.1	41.1
PSP								2.3						
Forward Bloc			6.9						**60.2**	**51.8**				
RCPI			32.5	**58.8**	**39.8**	37.8	14.3							
Jana Sangh			19.6					10.8		6.1				
HMS								1.5						
RRP								2.9						
Proutist				0.8									0.7	
Independents				0.3	8.6						1.5			
								1.5						
								1.1						
								0.8						
								0.4						

Howrah District	155. Shibpur							156. Dojmur						
	1952	1957	1962	1962	1969	1971	1972	1952	1957	1962	1967	1969	1971	1972
Congress			**37.5**	33.0	2.20	**54.7**		19.7	38.1	49.2	**48.6**	40.6	27.2	**49.9**
Congress (O)	(See	Howrah West)			6.9	1.4							3.2	1.6
Bangla Congress					1.3								7.7	
CPI								55.0	60.2	49.6				
CPM			27.6		**39.1**						47.2	**58.4**	**60.3**	48.5
PSP								0.4						
Forward Bloc			35.0	**67.0**	30.6	43.9		3.1						
Jana Sangh										1.2				
HMS								1.3						
INDF												0.3		
Proutist												0.7		
Independents								7.3	1.7		4.2		1.5	
								6.9						
								6.0						
								0.3						

Howrah District	157. Jagataballavpur							158. Panchla						
	1952	1957	1962	1967	1969	1971	1972	1952	1957	1962	1967	1969	1971	1972
Congress	**29.9**	41.6	**59.9**	41.0	39.5	24.5				48.29	**43.3**	35.7		**55.7**
Congress (O)						7.3	4.9						4.3	
Bangla Congress						3.6								
CPI							45.9							
CPM				49.2	**60.5**	56.9	49.2						**44.9**	40.9
PSP	8.6													
SSP						1.1								
Forward Bloc		**58.4**	40.1	9.8						**48.33**	26.2	**63.5**	40.5	
Jana Sangh	6.3													
Swatantra											3.4			
Proutist												0.8		0.3
Independents	18.5					6.6					27.3		10.3	0.7
	14.5									3.2				1.6
	13.5													0.6
	5.3													0.2
	3.4													

HOWRAH DISTRICT	159. SANKRAIL							160. ULUBERLA NORTH						
	1952	1957	1962	1967	1969	1971	1972	1952	1957	1962	1967	1969	1971	1972
Congress (1)	16.5	14.7	48.6	**50.7**	37.2	27.8	46.9	47.0	31.4	35.0	14.5		1.4	
Congress (2)	15.5	12.9												
Congress (O)						6.3						1.2		
CPI		**29.4**	**50.2**	16.4		13.5								
CPM				32.8	**61.0**	**52.3**	**53.1**			32.2		**52.1**	**53.9**	
PSP			1.2											
Forward Bloc (1)	**27.4**	**27.5**							53.0	36.4	65.0	32.2		
Forward Bloc (2)	**22.0**													
Jana Sangh	2.0													
RRP	1.2												41.2	
Proutist				1.8										
Independents	3.0	6.7											3.5	
	2.2	5.6												
	2.2	3.3												
	2.1													
	2.1													
	1.2													
	1.0													
	0.8													
	0.5													
	0.3													

HOWRAH DISTRICT	161. ULUBERIA SOUTH							162. SHYAMPUR						
	1952	1957	1962	1967	1969	1971	1972	1952	1957	1962	1967	1969	1971	1972
Congress		**54.2**	32.7	40.2	22.1		2.4	30.7	43.0	**55.2**	42.6	48.9	**38.5**	50.1
Congress (O)					4.2								3.6	1.0
CPM			24.8		**41.6**	45.9						23.2		
PSP		3.7						0.8						
Forward Bloc		38.5	**38.1**	**59.8**	20.3			51.0	54.5	43.8	**57.4**	**51.1**	34.7	48.9
Jana Sangh								0.9						
Proutist						0.6								
Independents		3.6	3.4			11.8	**46.4**	13.5	2.5	1.0				
			1.0				4.2	1.2						
							0.4	0.7						
								0.5						
								0.4						
								0.3						

HOWRAH DISTRICT	163. BAGNAN							164. KALYANPUR						
	1952	1957	1962	1967	1969	1971	1972	1952	1957	1962	1967	1969	1971	1972
Congress	**33.1**	37.3	**51.1**	**37.4**	38.5	33.2	**49.5**			39.7	41.1	24.7		
Congress (O)							2.7	(See Bagnan)					7.7	2.0
Bangla Congress				26.9		13.6					**46.0**	**56.8**	6.4		
CPI		**60.3**	46.0											**60.8**
CPM				35.8	**61.5**	**53.3**	47.2						**39.1**	37.2
PSP	7.7		0.9								1.6	2.1		
Forward Bloc	30.1									12.8			9.8	
Jana Sangh						0.6							8.7	
Independents	16.4	2.5	2.0										3.5	
	5.3													
	4.1													
	1.0													
	0.9													
	0.7													
	0.5													
	0.5													
	0.2													

HOWRAH DISTRICT	165. AMTA							166. UDAYNARAYANPUR						
	1952	1957	1962	1967	1969	1971	1972	1952	1957	1962	1967	1969	1971	1972
Congress			**51.6**	39.2	40.5	23.4	**50.2**			**50.2**	41.1	42.6	35.8	**56.3**
Congress (O)						4.3	2.7						4.3	
CPI		38.9												
CPM				**58.7**	**56.7**	**61.1**	47.1				**54.3**	**57.4**	**59.8**	43.7
PSP		5.0			11.2									
Forward Bloc			2.0							35.2	4.7			
Swatantra			4.5											
Proutist				2.9										
Jana Sangh										11.3				
SBP										1.8				
Independents										1.5				

HOWRAH DISTRICT	*Others :* HOWRAH EAST							*Others :* HOWRAH WEST						
	1952	1957	1962	1967	1969	1971	1972	1952	1957	1962	1967	1969	1971	1972
Congress	**56.6**	**47.4**	**48.8**	(See				**34.6**	**39.2**	39.4	(See			
CPI		44.6	48.6	Howrah							Howrah			
PSP	1.9		1.0			Central)			37.1				South)	
Forward Bloc								22.0						
RCPI								6.5						
Jana Sangh	1.3		1.6					6.4						
Independents	38.8	4.2						22.5	20.2	**44.6**				
	0.9	3.8						3.8	3.5	16.0				
	0.6							1.7						
								1.3						
								0.6						
								0.6						

HOWRAH DISTRICT	*Others :* ULUBERIA							*Others :* AMTA SOUTH						
	1952	1957	1962	1967	1969	1971	1972	1952	1957	1962	1967	1969	1971	1972
Congress (1)	20.6	**25.7**						**36.1**						
Congress (2)	18.8	23.3												
CPI			(See Uluberia					27.3		(See Amta East)				
PSP	2.7				North			14.6						
Forward Bloc (1)	29.8	24.4			and									
Forward Bloc (2)	**20.7**	**26.6**				South)								
Jana Sangh								6.3						
Independents	7.3							14.8						
	2.9							0.9						
	2.2													

HOWRAH DISTRICT	*Others* : AMTA CENTRAL							*Others* : AMTA NORTH						
	1952	1957	1962	1967	1969	1971	1972	1952	1957	1962	1967	1969	1971	1972
Congress	**36.9**							28.1						
CPI	0.9	(See Amta West)						(See Amta)						
PSP	25.5							14.7						
Forward Bloc	20.2													
Jana Sangh	2.7													
Independents	8.3							**53.6**						
	2.7							2.2						
	1.4							1.3						
	1.3													

HOWRAH DISTRICT	*Others* : AMTA EAST							*Others* : AMTA WEST						
	1952	1957	1962	1967	1969	1971	1972	1952	1957	1962	1967	1969	1971	1972
Congress	47.5							**42.5**						
CPI	(See Amta South)							(See Amta Central)						
PSP	**52.5**													
Forward Bloc								19.0						
Jana Sangh								10.5						
Independents								28.0						

HOOGHLY DISTRICT	167. JANGIPARA							168. CHANDITALA						
	1952	1957	1962	1967	1969	1971	1972	1952	1957	1962	1967	1969	1971	1972
Congress (1)	**23.5**	**47.2**	41.7	40.5	30.1	**51.6**		48.2	26.5	31.8	20.3	**54.2**		
Congress (2)	**25.3**													
Congress (O)												8.4		
Bangla Congress			14.2		11.7									
CPI	21.7	42.8			9.2			46.8	7.4					
CPM			44.2	57.6	**49.0**	48.4				22.3		**49.4**	45.8	
PSP	12.8	3.7								5.0				
Forward Bloc												6.4		
INDF				1.8										
HMS	8.6													
Independents	6.9	6.3								37.7	68.2	9.9		
	1.2										6.2	5.6		

Hooghly District	169. UTTARPARA							170. SERAMPORE						
	1952	1957	1962	1967	1969	1971	1972	1952	1957	1962	1967	1969	1971	1972
Congress	34.2	39.3	44.3	38.9	37.0			**44.0**	44.5	48.3	**55.6**	43.1	**45.3**	**60.6**
Congress (O)						11.5							2.2	1.9
CPI	**52.4**	**56.7**	**53.2**	11.7		32.4	49.993	41.4	**52.6**	**51.7**	42.3	**53.6**	15.5	
CPM				**47.4**	**61.2**	**56.1**	50.007						36.9	37.5
PSP	1.2							0.8						
Forward Bloc	1.2							3.0						
Jana Sangh					1.8									
HMS		4.1	2.5											
Proutist												0.4		
Independents	1.9			2.1				9.8	2.2		2.1	2.9		
	5.0							0.7	0.8					
	4.2							0.3						

Hooghly District	171. CHAMPDANI							172. CHANDERNAGORE						
	1952	1957	1962	1967	1969	1971	1972	1952	1957	1962	1967	1969	1971	1972
Congress	(See Bhadreswar)		**53.4**	41.3	26.7			44.9	48.0	42.4	39.8	32.8	49.3	
Congress (O)					4.3	1.9						3.5		
CPI			16.3		21.1	**51.3**			**50.0**					
CPM			28.8	**58.7**	**47.8**	46.3				**54.9**	**58.0**	**54.8**	**49.4**	
PSP									2.0					
Jana Sangh						0.5					1.2			
Proutist											1.0			
Independents			1.6					**51.9**		1.6		8.4	1.3	
								3.2		1.1		0.4		

HOOGHLY DISTRICT	173. SINGUR							174. HARIPAL						
	1952	1957	1962	1967	1969	1971	1972	1952	1957	1962	1967	1969	1971	1972
Congress (1)	17.7	**52.5**	**50.2**	**48.3**	42.0						37.9	37.9	37.2	48.9
Congress (2)	16.6													
Congress (O)						14.6	4.9			(See Singur)			6.0	
Bangla Congress						2.0								
CPI (1)	**19.7**	45.9	49.8	24.7		**43.9**	**55.9**							
CPI (2)	**16.7**													
CPM				27.0	**58.0**	39.5	39.2							
PSP	3.5											1.5		
Forward Bloc											18.1			
Worker's Party													**49.9**	**50.9**
SSP											**44.0**	**46.8**	7.0	
Jana Sangh	8.4													
Independents	5.0	1.6										13.3		0.3
	4.4											0.6		
	3.9													
	3.9													

HOOGHLY DISTRICT	175. CHINSURAH							176. POLBA						
	1952	1957	1962	1967	1969	1971	1972	1952	1957	1962	1967	1969	1971	1972
Congress (1)	**19.4**	**56.8**	42.0	39.7	33.9	**44.1**	**53.7**				**56.7**	43.2	38.7	**54.9**
Congress (2)	17.2													
Congress (O)						1.3							5.9	
Bangla Congress													2.8	
CPI														
CPM						43.6					40.7	**51.5**	**46.6**	43.4
PSP (1)	5.3													
PSP (2)	6.4													
Forward Bloc (1)	**18.4**	40.6	**55.0**	**58.6**	**64.7**	11.3	45.0						3.6	
Forward Bloc (2)	15.6													
Jana Sangh				1.8	0.8							2.6		
HMS	7.1													
INDF					0.2							1.2		
Independents	8.6	2.6	3.0		0.4	0.9					2.3	2.4	1.6	
	1.1										1.8			
	0.6													

HOOGHLY DISTRICT

	177. BALAGARH							178. PANDUA						
	1952	1957	1962	1967	1969	1971	1972	1952	1957	1962	1967	1969	1971	1972
Congress	**35.3**	44.9	**56.4**	**45.2**	39.6	39.2	**54.9**			**55.7**	**45.2**	41.5		**59.0**
Congress (O)					1.0									
Bangla Congress			9.7								15.7		35.6	
CPI		**47.6**	35.6			10.2				33.8				
CPM				45.1	**60.4**	**47.5**	45.1				37.7	**57.9**	**56.4**	41.0
PSP	23.3													
Forward Bloc	22.8													
INDF												0.6		
HMS	3.7	7.6												
Independents	6.8		8.0			2.0				6.3	1.5		6.3	
	5.2									4.2			1.7	
	2.1													
	0.9													

HOOGHLY DISTRICT

	179. DHANIAKALI							180. TARAKESWAR						
	1952	1957	1962	1967	1969	1971	1972	1952	1957	1962	1967	1969	1971	1972
Congress (1)	**20.0**	**25.7**	**45.4**	40.7	43.8	39.4	**56.0**	47.1	**72.0**	**50.0**	37.3	47.7	26.2	**54.3**
Congress (2)	**19.9**	**27.4**												
Congress (O)													10.6	
Bangla Congress					6.6									
CPI								22.6		40.0				
CPM			11.7		**46.4**	44.0								
PSP (1)	4.9		0.6					18.9	28.0	5.0				
PSP (2)	4.0							1.4						
Forward Bloc (1)	10.6			**47.6**	**56.3**	7.5							1.3	
Forward Bloc (2)	10.4													
Forward Bloc (M)											**51.8**	**55.7**	45.7	
Jana Sangh (1)	11.4													
Jana Sangh (2)	8.6													
HMS	7.7	12.7								5.0				
Proutist												0.5		
Independents	1.4	16.4	40.0					10.0			**62.7**		6.1	
	1.1	16.0	14.0											
		1.8												

Hooghly District	181. Pursurah							182. Khanakul						
	1952	1957	1962	1967	1969	1971	1972	1952	1957	1962	1967	1969	1971	1972
Congress (1)				**54.1**	**52.2**	**42.4**	**64.2**	**35.8**	**60.5**		35.8	43.5	33.0	**60.7**
Congress (2)								**33.9**						
Congress (O)						12.6							8.0	3.4
Bangla Congress							4.8						13.6	
CPI					46.4	18.2		17.8	28.0					
CPM				41.5		26.8					**64.2**	**53.7**	**41.8**	35.9
Forward Bloc								12.5					3.7	
Forward Bloc (M)							31.0							
INDF					1.3									
Lok Dal													2.8	
Independents				2.3, 2.1					11.5					

Hooghly District	183. Arambagh							184. Goghat						
	1952	1957	1962	1967	1969	1971	1972	1952	1957	1962	1967	1969	1971	1972
Congress (1)	18.2	**72.3**	(See Arambagh East)	48.3	**61.9**		26.6	23.1			31.7	45.9	**30.9**	**51.1**
Congress (2)	15.4													
Congress (O)						**60.6**	55.1	(See Arambagh West)					15.9	4.9
Bangla Congress				**49.9**	36.7									
CPI	25.2													
CPM						29.7	18.2						24.1	
Forward Bloc		17.7				3.7		3.2			**66.0**	**54.1**	23.9	42.4
Jana Sangh								0.5						
HMS		4.2												
Independents	**34.2**, 4.7, 2.3	3.4, 2.3		1.9	0.8, 0.4, 0.3	6.0		**62.4**, 6.2, 1.5, 1.4, 1.1, 0.8			2.3		5.1	1.6

HOOGHLY DISTRICT	*Others:* ARAMBAGH EAST							*Others:* ARAMBAGH WEST						
	1952	1957	1962	1967	1969	1971	1972	1952	1957	1962	1967	1969	1971	1972
Congress			**69.2**							**50.3**				
Forward Bloc			30.0 (See Arambagh)							18.0 (See Goghat)				
Independents			0.8							25.0				
										6.7				

HOOGHLY DISTRICT	*Others:* BHADRESWAR						
	1952	1957	1962	1967	1969	1971	1972
Congress	**51.2**	**55.5**	42.7				
CPI			**52.3** (See Champdani)				
PSP	2.6	3.0					
Forward Bloc	44.3						
SBP		2.0					
RRP	1.9						
Independents		44.5	0.1				

MIDNAPORE DISTRICT	185. CHANDRAKONA							186. GHATAL						
	1952	1957	1962	1967	1969	1971	1972	1952	1957	1962	1967	1969	1971	1972
Congress (1)			**53.8**	**39.2**	43.1	29.5		16.5	**30.0**	41.0	32.3	36.4		**52.4**
Congress (2)	(See							9.9	**25.0**					
Congress (O)	Ghatal)				4.5	1.8								2.9
Bangla Congress			22.9								23.7		37.7	
CPI (1)			46.2			23.5	53.4	**26.0**	18.0	**59.0**				
CPI (2)								**23.9**	22.0					
CPM				29.7	**56.9**	**42.5**	43.2				**44.1**	**63.6**	**59.4**	47.6
PSP (1)								10.3						
PSP (2)								9.0						
Jana Sangh (1)								2.2						
Jana Sangh (2)								2.2						
HMS									5.0					
Independents				8.2		1.6								

MIDNAPORE DISTRICT	187. DASPUR							188. PANSKURA WEST						
	1952	1957	1962	1967	1969	1971	1972	1952	1957	1962	1967	1969	1971	1972
Congress	35.5	**57.0**	39.1	**50.2**	47.1	**44.9**	**58.9**	**56.3**	**54.1**	36.7	43.8	23.3		
Congress (O)					5.7								7.9	12.4
Bangla Congress										**63.3**	**56.2**	13.5		
CPI	**36.8**	37.0	**52.2**		11.3			41.0	45.9				**39.2**	**66.0**
CPM				42.7	**52.9**	37.6	38.9						12.0	21.6
PSP	2.5													
HMS		2.0	7.7											
SBP			1.0											
Independents	22.0	2.1		5.9		0.4	2.3	2.7					4.0	
	3.2	1.9		1.3										

MIDNAPORE DISTRICT	189. PANSKURA EAST							190. MOYNA						
	1952	1957	1962	1967	1969	1971	1972	1952	1957	1962	1967	1969	1971	1972
Congress		**55.5**	**52.4**	27.9	36.2			40.6	**48.8**	**50.2**	30.2	40.9	29.4	
Congress (O)						12.6							5.8	8.7
Bangla Congress						15.9								
CPI		44.5	47.6	**63.4**	**63.8**	54.4	**72.2**	51.8	37.8	48.0	**65.9**	**59.1**	41.0	**59.9**
CPM						13.9						3.9	23.9	31.4
PSP											7.6			
Forward Bloc						27.8								
RSP					3.3									
HMS										3.5	1.8			
Independents					7.1					10.0				
					1.6									

	191. Tamluk							192. Mahishadal						
Midnapore District	1952	1957	1962	1967	1969	1971	1972	1952	1957	1962	1967	1969	1971	1972
Congress (1)	**47.2**	**57.6**	**52.0**	18.3	23.9		**74.5**	18.3	21.8	**53.0**	28.9	35.2	9.5	**62.8**
Congress (2)										22.5				
Congress (O)						5.6							2.3	
Bangla Congress				**81.7**	**76.1**	**63.8**					**71.1**	**64.8**	**47.2**	
CPI	39.8	42.4	48.0										24.2	
CPM						24.4	24.3						12.8	17.0
PSP (1)	4.7										22.5			
PSP (2)											20.7			
Forward Bloc											16.8			
Jana Sangh	8.3													
HMS (1)									4.4					
HMS (2)									4.1					
Independents						4.4	1.2	4.1	47.0				4.0	20.0
						1.7	**65.0**							

	193. Sutahata							194. Nandigram						
Midnapore District	1952	1957	1962	1967	1969	1971	1972	1952	1957	1962	1967	1969	1971	1972
Congress	33.8		**56.7**	43.1	**50.4**	12.2					40.7	43.5	2.3	
Congress (O)						13.4		(See					24.0	39.4
Bangla Congress			**52.7**	49.6	**35.1**			Nandigram					14.8	
CPI	1.3					24.8	**50.2**	South)			**58.6**	**56.5**	**42.5**	**46.3**
CPM						14.5	25.8							12.5
PSP	**55.4**		31.0											
Forward Bloc			12.3											
HMS	9.6													
Muslim League														1.7
Independents				4.3			24.0				0.8		9.4	
													7.0	

(Sutahata 1957 column: "(See Mahishadal)")

MIDNAPORE DISTRICT	195. NARGHAT							196. BHAGABANPUR						
	1952	1957	1962	1967	1969	1971	1972	1952	1957	1962	1967	1969	1971	1972
Congress (1)			39.5	**52.7**	19.9	**57.3**	25.1	**26.2**	**65.5**	**48.9**	**52.2**		15.3	**43.8**
Congress (2)									23.2					
Congress (O)	(See				22.0								23.9	19.9
Bangla Congress	Nandigram		**60.5**	47.3	**26.0**					44.3	47.8	23.4		
CPI	North)				25.8				15.5					
CPM						24.9							**25.3**	32.7
PSP (1)								26.4	**24.8**	19.0				
PSP (2)								12.4	22.0					
SSP												6.8		
Jana Sangh								**31.5**	3.8					
Socialist														2.8
Independents					6.3	17.8		4.7	2.0				6.3	0.8
													4.2	
													1.7	

MIDNAPORE DISTRICT	197. KHAJURI							198. CONTAI NORTH						
	1952	1957	1962	1967	1969	1971	1972	1952	1957	1962	1967	1969	1971	1972
Congress (1)	**20.9**		**65.6**	**39.7**	45.7		**61.7**	24.8	49.9	**54.2**	**44.5**	41.8	26.3	
Congress (2)	**19.1**													
Congress (O)					27.2	8.3							12.2	14.8
Bangla Congress				34.3	**46.6**	12.4								
CPI								17.3		25.9				**50.8**
CPM					**31.6**	25.9					13.0		21.8	25.2
PSP (1)	16.2		34.4					**35.3**	**50.1**	19.9	42.5	**58.3**	30.6	
PSP (2)	10.7							3.4						
PSP (3)	9.2													
PSP (4)	7.1													
SSP				25.4	7.7	9.2								
Socialist								2.6						9.1
Forward Bloc	13.6													
Jana Sangh			0.7					15.3						
Independents	2.3					19.6		1.6	4.2				9.1	
	0.9													

(Note: Khajuri column carries the vertical note "(See Bhagabanpur)")

MIDNAPORE DISTRICT	199. CONTAI SOUTH							200. RAMNAGAR						
	1952	1957	1962	1967	1969	1971	1972	1952	1957	1962	1967	1969	1971	1972
Congress	24.1	**48.1**	48.6	45.7	42.9	10.2		**36.5**	**56.5**	48.4	**54.5**	44.4	23.2	**55.6**
Congress (O)						29.1	43.5						**26.0**	11.4
Bangla Congress													21.1	
CPM						10.5	12.6							19.8
PSP	**40.1**	45.4	**51.4**	**51.0**	**57.1**	**38.6**		36.5	43.6	**51.6**	43.7	**54.7**		
SSP				2.1							1.7			
Socialist	14.6													4.7
Jana Sangh	21.1	4.3						19.5						
Proutist												0.9		
Independents		2.2		1.2		8.1	**43.9**	7.5					16.5	8.5
						3.4							13.2	

MIDNAPORE DISTRICT	201. EGRA							202. MUGBERIA						
	1952	1957	1962	1967	1969	1971	1972	1952	1957	1962	1967	1969	1971	1972
Congress	41.9	**69.5**	38.0	37.2	11.9	**43.2**				34.5	44.9			**51.5**
Congress (O)					11.5			(See				**26.5**		1.1
Bangla Congress					8.4			Pataspur)		**52.0**	**55.1**	5.6		
CPM					**14.2**	**14.5**						**30.0**		29.8
PSP	**44.6**	30.5	**62.0**	**62.8**	**41.8**							27.8		
SSP										13.5		10.1		
Socialist						42.3								17.7
Jana Sangh	8.7													
Independents	4.7				12.1									

MIDNAPORE DISTRICT	203. PATASPUR							204. PINGLA						
	1952	1957	1962	1967	1969	1971	1972	1952	1957	1962	1967	1969	1971	1972
Congress	24.7	38.9	**52.4**	45.6	48.8	**44.3**	**72.1**	23.2			42.8	45.1	**45.9**	**58.6**
Congress (O)						7.6			(See				2.3	
Bangla Congress									Sabang)				3.7	
CPI				**54.4**	**51.2**	38.5					**55.2**	**54.1**	24.4	
CPM							27.9							
PSP	3.6	**52.4**	27.6					26.0						
Jana Sangh	**71.7**	8.7						**27.0**			2.1			
Jharkhand													1.9	0.9
Proutist												0.8		
Independents			20.0			9.6		23.8					21.8	40.5

MIDNAPORE DISTRICT	205. DEBRA							206. KESHPUR						
	1952	1957	1962	1967	1969	1971	1972	1952	1957	1962	1967	1969	1971	1972
Congress (1)	**53.4**	**38.6**	36.6	**50.2**	36.6	**59.9**	13.2	**55.0**		**47.4**	47.2	**42.9**		**57.8**
Congress (2)							14.1							
Congress (O)					4.9							1.3		
Bangla Congress			**47.9**	49.8	6.3					28.0	**52.8**	5.3		
CPI (1)		19.1			11.6		**15.7**	45.0				18.8		
CPI (2)							13.5							
CPM			15.5		33.4	37.3				24.6		31.6		39.7
PSP (1)	39.0	24.0					**15.2**							
PSP (2)							12.4							
Jana Sangh	5.7	4.3												
Jharkhand					1.9	1.8								2.5
SBP		14.0												
Independents	1.9				3.2	0.9	11.6							
					2.0		2.2							
							2.1							

MIDNAPORE DISTRICT	207. GARHBETTA EAST							208. GARHBETTA WEST						
	1952	1957	1962	1967	1969	1971	1972	1952	1957	1962	1967	1969	1971	1972
Congress				**49.9**	37.3	30.0					**46.2**	33.4	22.1	
Congress (O)	(See Garhbetta)					6.9	7.5	(See Garhbetta)					12.7	1.3
Bangla Congress				34.0		3.1							2.9	
CPI					**57.0**	**33.5**	**54.9**				41.8	**57.9**	**27.2**	**53.2**
CPM				16.2		26.6	35.1				7.3		24.8	33.8
Jana Sangh											1.5			
Lok Dal					5.7							1.7		
Jharkhand							2.5					3.1		9.6
Independents											3.3	4.0	10.2	2.2

MIDNAPORE DISTRICT	209. SALBANI							210. MIDNAPUR						
	1952	1957	1962	1967	1969	1971	1972	1952	1957	1962	1967	1969	1971	1972
Congress	29.2	**39.9**	30.5	30.2		13.0		**41.4**	**39.4**	37.2	43.7		42.3	
Congress (O)						6.7							1.5	
Bangla Congress			**40.3**	**55.3**		14.0							1.6	
CPI		26.5				20.1	**48.2**	28.0	36.4	**56.3**	**54.3**		**46.4**	**77.0**
CPM			16.8			**26.4**	36.7							19.0
PSP		1.8							11.0					
Forward Bloc	19.3													
Jana Sangh								18.6	2.2	6.5				
HMS		24.2		1.7					11.0		1.4			
Lok Dal				4.4							0.6			
Jharkhand						14.8	15.1						1.6	2.6
Independents	35.5	7.0	7.4	8.3		3.0		10.3					6.7	1.4
	12.0	0.6	3.4			1.9		1.7						
	4.0		1.6											

MIDNAPORE DISTRICT	211. KHARAGPUR							212. KHARAGPUR LOCAL						
	1952	1957	1962	1967	1969	1971	1972	1952	1957	1962	1967	1969	1971	1972
Congress (1)	46.5	35.6	39.1	44.3	54.9	60.2	79.0	30.1	54.3	44.1	48.4		38.9	62.0
Congress (2)								28.6						
Congress (O)						1.4							2.2	
Bangla Congress						1.1							1.5	
CPI		57.9	52.0	49.0	44.0	23.1		17.2	39.8	55.9	51.6		38.9	
CPM				6.7		14.2	21.0						17.0	35.3
PSP (1)	8.4		4.4					14.4	4.9					
PSP (2)	1.5													
Jan Sangh (1)	30.2	2.2	0.2		0.5			5.4						
Jan Sangh (2)								4.3						
HMS									1.0					
INDF					0.5									
Jharkhand													1.5	2.8
Independents	11.6	4.4	4.3		0.2									
	1.8													

MIDNAPORE DISTRICT	213. NARAYANGARH							214. DANTAN						
	1952	1957	1962	1967	1969	1971	1972	1952	1957	1962	1967	1969	1971	1972
Congress (1)	17.0		63.3	52.5	48.0	48.0	71.9	27.8	57.4	60.1	45.2	48.2	17.0	
Congress (2)	16.3													
Congress (O)						4.9							31.4	47.2
Bangla Congress				46.2	49.8	15.4	4.5				54.8	51.8	9.3	
CPI		(See Kharagpur Local)	25.2			20.9							31.9	38.1
CPM							23.6							14.7
PSP (1)	16.9		11.5							7.6				
PSP (2)	8.0													
PSP (3)	5.9													
Jana Sangh	23.9							72.2						
INDF					2.2									
Jharkhand						1.6							2.5	
Independents	7.4			1.3		9.1			32.5	32.3			7.8	
	4.6								10.1					

215. Keshiari · 216. Nayagram — Midnapore District

MIDNAPORE DISTRICT	215. Keshiari							216. Nayagram						
	1952	1957	1962	1967	1969	1971	1972	1952	1957	1962	1967	1969	1971	1972
Congress				**50.4**	**54.3**	**41.7**	**53.8**			49.9	24.8	36.1	**38.4**	**49.1**
Congress (O)						2.7		(See Gopiballavpur)					1.6	
Bangla Congress				45.1	43.5	2.8					**40.3**	**60.0**	4.5	
CPI						15.9								
CPM						30.0	41.4						23.5	
PSP										26.7				
SSP											29.8		12.0	
Socialist														32.5
Lok Dal												4.0		
Jharkhand					2.3	6.8	3.4						19.6	17.4
Independents				4.5			1.4			10.2	5.1			1.0
										6.4			0.3	
										4.9				
										2.0				

217. Gopiballavpur · 218. Jhargram — Midnapore District

MIDNAPORE DISTRICT	217. Gopiballavpur							218. Jhargram						
	1952	1957	1962	1967	1969	1971	1972	1952	1957	1962	1967	1969	1971	1972
Congress (1)	18.1	**27.0**	**48.6**	39.4	40.1	**31.8**	**57.6**	19.8	**46.5**	**43.5**	40.5	40.8	**38.8**	**52.3**
Congress (2)	12.6	**21.5**						16.4						
Congress (O)						13.8							3.5	
Bangla Congress												**46.7**	3.9	
CPI													7.7	
CPM						28.5	37.3						31.6	29.5
PSP (1)	**27.3**	16.0	37.3						11.5	41.5	36.3			
PSP (2)	**16.8**	13.0												
PSP (3)	6.7													
SSP				**60.6**	**52.2**	13.5								
Socialist														2.0
Forward Bloc										6.6				
RSP										9.0			2.1	
Lok Dal												8.2		
Jana Sangh (1)								18.3						
Jana Sangh (2)								15.5						
HMS										0.9				
Proutist					1.1									
Jharkhand Party					3.8	6.9	3.8						12.3	14.7
Independents	10.2	7.0	6.1		2.5		1.3	8.8	7.5	10.8	**59.5**	4.2		1.4
	8.4	6.3	4.1			3.2		3.2	4.5					
		6.3	3.9			2.2								
		3.0												

MIDNAPORE DISTRICT	219. BINPUR							Others : SABANG						
	1952	1957	1962	1967	1969	1971	1972	1952	1957	1962	1967	1969	1971	1972
Congress (1)	14.8	15.7	**48.7**	**40.1**	35.8	30.4		**37.0**	**50.4**	**53.1**				
Congress (2)	**11.0**	13.5												
Congress (O)					3.7									
Bangla Congress					2.5									
CPI (1)			**18.2**	22.5	26.8	**44.5**	20.1	**57.2**	3.0	11.2				
CPI (2)			**13.8**											
CPM					11.1									
PSP (1)	12.1		19.5					18.0						
PSP (2)	9.5							8.2						
PSP (3)	6.7													
PSP (4)	6.1													
SSP				14.9										
Forward Bloc	6.6													
Lok Dal				2.7										
Jana Sangh	**15.5**	9.5							35.7					
HMS		11.7	3.3											
Jharkhand					17.0	**32.2**	35.9							
Socialist						5.5								
Independents	10.5	7.9	6.0	14.4				1.4	33.8	2.7	46.9			
	4.9	4.3		3.8										
	2.5	5.5												

MIDNAPORE DISTRICT	Others : PANSKURA NORTH							Others : PANSKURA SOUTH						
	1952	1957	1962	1957	1969	1971	1972	1952	1947	1962	1967	1969	1971	1972
Congress	**61.0**							**59.2**						
CPI	32.9	(See Panskura East)						29.3	(See Panskura West)					
PSP	6.2							11.5						

MIDNAPORE DISTRICT	*Others :* GARHBETTA							*Others :* MOHANPUR						
	1952	1957	1962	1967	1969	1971	1972	1952	1957	1962	1967	1969	1971	1972
Congress (1)	18.7	17.5	**59.9**	(See Garhbetta)				33.8	(See Egra)					
Congress (2)		**18.6**		East										
CPI (1)	**28.3**	20.7	34.2	and										
CPI (2)		16.2		West)										
PSP (1)	14.1							19.2						
PSP (2)	4.1							4.2						
Jana Sangh (1)	17.4	7.2						**42.9**						
Jana Sangh (2)		3.7												
Independents	13.9	6.9	4.6											
	3.4	5.7	1.3											
		1.9												
		1.4												

MIDNAPORE DISTRICT	*Others :* NANDIGRAM NORTH							*Others :* NANDIGRAM SOUTH						
	1952	1957	1962	1967	1969	1971	1972	1952	1957	1962	1967	1969	1971	1972
Congress	**43.5**	**58.5**	55.1	(See Narghat)				**39.7**	47.8	**58.5**				
CPI	3.0								38.8	**52.2**	41.5	(See Nandigram)		
PSP	31.7		4.9					13.9						
Forward Bloc		41.5												
Jana Sangh								7.7						
Independents	21.8		40.0											

PURULIA DISTRICT	220. BANDUAN							221. MANBAZAR						
	1952	1957	1962	1967	1969	1971	1972	1952	1957	1962	1967	1969	1971	1972
Congress (1)			43.2	36.5	**46.2**	**33.3**	**53.6**	19.2	19.0	33.2	36.9	**47.2**		**51.9**
Congress (2)								19.1						
Congress (O)					7.7	5.4							3.6	
Bangla Congress													6.7	
CPI				8.2						13.8				
CPM							34.3							48.1
SUC													9.7	
INDF				1.1								7.4		
Lok Sevak Sangh (1)	**56.8**	**52.1**	42.4	31.7				**30.9**	**46.6**	**50.2**	**47.2**	32.0		
Lok Sevak Sangh (2)								**30.8**						
Jana Sangh			2.5	7.1	9.2						3.1	8.4	5.7	
Swatantra			8.9								13.6			
Jharkhand					9.9	6.7								
Independents				3.2					20.6					

PURULIA DISTRICT	222. BALARAMPUR							223. ARSA						
	1952	1957	1962	1967	1969	1971	1972	1952	1957	1962	1967	1969	1971	1972
Congress	25.8	21.6	23.3	34.0	35.0	**54.2**		19.7	31.0	**32.3**	34.2	**36.3**		**50.4**
Congress (O)													13.2	
Bangla Congress													8.6	
CPI	13.7	32.5												
CPM			27.4		**39.3**	45.8							12.2	
SSP					2.6									
Forward Bloc									**33.0**	18.0	**47.3**	26.5		49.6
Lok Sevak Sangh	**41.2**	**33.9**	**38.8**	**56.2**	15.9				9.0					
SUC									12.0					
Jana Sangh			8.4	9.8	7.2						1.5			
Lok Dal												13.9		
INDF												3.9		
HMS													0.7	0.8
Swatantra										21.6				
Independents	11.4	8.1	2.1					**26.4**	10.0	14.5			2.4	
	5.3	3.9						12.4	4.9	6.4				
	2.7							5.9		2.7				
								6.3		1.1				
								5.8		1.0				
								5.6		0.9				
								5.0						
								5.0						
								4.0						
								3.9						

PURULIA District	224. JHALDA							225. JAIPUR						
	1952	1957	1962	1967	1969	1971	1972	1952	1957	1962	1967	1969	1971	1972
Congress		**49.0**	**51.7**	46.7	**51.5**	**46.7**	**51.9**	40.0	**32.9**	**38.3**	**50.0**	**66.9**		
Congress (O)					4.4								8.9	
Bangla Congress													14.6	
CPI		15.0							8.0					
CPM					16.8									
PSP												16.9	12.4	
Socialist														15.8
Forward Bloc				**52.0**	48.5	31.0	48.1							17.4
Lok Sevak Sangh	35.8	28.0				1.2		**48.6**	15.1	38.0	12.6			
Jana Sangh			1.3							5.7	6.8			
Swatantra										18.0				
Independents	8.5	2.8						3.0	10.8				1.6	
	3.4	2.5						0.2	7.8					
	3.3							0.1	5.4					
									3.1					
									1.3					

PURULIA District	226. PURULIA							227. PARA						
	1952	1957	1962	1967	1969	1971	1972	1952	1957	1962	1967	1969	1971	1972
Congress (1)	14.5	**45.9**	28.9	27.2	**46.5**	**65.8**		**45.8**	36.0	33.8		**38.6**	**52.4**	
Congress (2)	14.4													
Congress (O)													5.5	1.3
Bangla Congress										**40.3**	**99.2**	10.5		
CPI		18.0			12.0									
CPM						34.2							18.8	
Forward Bloc								15.0						
Forward Block (M)					6.7									
SUC													25.2	42.4
Lok Sevak Sangh (1)	**25.4**	33.0	**48.5**	**63.1**	30.6			34.0				1.4		
Lok Sevak Sangh (2)	**20.8**													
Lok Dal					4.8							3.4		
Proutist												3.7		
INDF												2.1		
Jana Sangh			3.9		4.1						17.9	8.7		
Independents	8.7	2.1	8.1	5.0				3.5	5.9			4.1		3.9
	4.8	1.0	5.1					1.7						
	4.5		2.0											
	3.6		1.9											
	3.2		1.2											
			0.4											

PURULIA DISTRICT	228. RAGHUNATHPUR							229. KASHIPUR						
	1952	1957	1962	1967	1969	1971	1972	1952	1957	1962	1967	1969	1971	1972
Congress (1)	**26.2**	**54.3**	**46.3**	18.8	28.4	**50.7**		**21.0**	**52.5**	**43.6**	30.3	**38.5**	**57.3**	
Congress (2)	**21.1**							20.0						
Congress (O)					6.6							5.3		
Bangla Congress					5.9							7.5		
CPI										42.4	**61.6**	22.1		
CPM					24.5							21.6	40.9	
Forward Bloc		11.0							· 7.9					
SUC					**74.1**	**32.8**	49.3							
Lok Sevak Sangh		17.4	13.6	38.6		1.8		**20.1**	26.8			5.0		
INDF				3.2								5.5		
Jana Sangh			5.2	2.4						13.9				
HMS	6.3													
Independents	15.3	9.2	9.9	1.6				19.1	6.8		0.6		2.7	
	10.4	7.8						12.4	6.0		2.0			
	3.4	3.0						7.4						
		1.1												

PURULIA DISTRICT	230. HURA						
	1952	1957	1962	1967	1969	1971	1972
Congress		·	**40.6**	31.8	39.0	**46.0**	53.6
Congress (O)					5.8		
Bangla Congress					9.7		
CPM					17.2		
SUC					8.0	40.9	
Lok Sevak Sangh			35.1	**33.5**	**40.0**	13.3	
Lok Dal					5.7		
Jan Sangh			·	9.2	4.1		
Independents		·	18.0	14.1	11.3		5.5
			6.3	11.3			

| | 231. TALDANGRA | | | | | | | 232. RAIPUR | | | | | | |
BANKURA DISTRICT	1952	1957	1962	1967	1969	1971	1972	1952	1957	1962	1967	1969	1971	1972
Congress (1)	**29.1**		**55.8**	**57.4**	42.0	41.0	**54.8**	14.9	17.8	47.0	42.2	43.8	21.3	
Congress (2)									**14.2**					
Congress (O)					3.4								8.3	6.1
Bangla Congress										51.5	46.0	18.3		
CPI		35.3			4.3			6.1	3.9				17.1	**62.2**
CPM				42.7	**47.7**	**45.7**	40.9							
PSP (1)	8.4							11.2	7.3	31.2				
PSP (2)								3.9						
Forward Bloc (1)	4.2							3.8						
Forward Bloc (2)								2.9						
Lok Dal				1.7										
Jana Sangh	24.6										6.4			
HMS (1)			4.9		0.8				6.4					
HMS (2)									4.9					
Jharkhand						5.5	4.3						**21.4**	30.3
Independents	20.5		5.0		4.4			**15.5**	7.3	12.2			10.3	13.6	1.4
	10.1				3.4			10.5	7.1	7.8				
	3.4							13.8	6.9	2.0				
								9.8	6.0					
								7.6	5.5					
								4.9						
								3.5						
								2.9						
								1.6						

(See Raipur) — note under TALDANGRA 1957 column.

| | 233. RANIBANDH | | | | | | | 234. INDUPUR | | | | | | |
BANKURA DISTRICT	1952	1957	1962	1967	1969	1971	1972	1952	1957	1962	1967	1969	1971	1972
Congress			24.3	**52.1**	44.4	12.5	**49.5**	(See Chhatna)		**46.6**	**55.4**	37.3	17.1	**57.3**
Congress (O)					6.1								6.5	
Bangla Congress					21.7					30.6	**61.6**	28.2		3.3
CPI			**54.7**		4.0							13.5		
CPM				23.1	**51.3**	**50.4**	45.8							
PSP											4.7			
RSP													5.2	
INDF					1.5								0.8	
Jana Sangh				4.7								9.3		
HMS										37.5				
Jharkhand						5.3	4.7							
Independents			20.0	16.9	2.9					15.9			**29.4**	39.4
			1.0	3.3										

235. Chhatna · 236. Gangajalghati

Bankura District	235. Chhatna							236. Gangajalghati						
	1952	1957	1962	1967	1969	1971	1972	1952	1957	1962	1967	1969	1971	1972
Congress (1)	**16.5**	**30.9**	**56.3**	**49.5**	44.4	**45.0**	50.4	43.8	50.2	43.5	41.4	30.0		**59.0**
Congress (2)	19.6	**26.1**												
Congress (O)						17.6	9.0					4.8		
Bangla Congress			4.9			18.4				56.6	54.5	16.7		
CPI	6.6													
CPM												48.5		41.0
PSP								7.6						
SSP				33.8	**48.0**	3.7								
Forward Bloc	9.5													
Socialist							4.9							
SUC						11.8	35.7							
INDF				3.8							4.0			
Lok Dal				2.4										
Proutist				1.4										
Jana Sangh								28.1						
HMS	**21.8**	16.1							49.8					
Independents	12.1	14.0	40.0	6.1		3.5		20.5						
	6.9	4.7	3.7	2.9										
	5.1	4.3	1.8											
	2.0	3.9												

Gangajalghati 1971: (See Chhatna)

237. Barjora · 238. Bankura

Bankura District	237. Barjora							238. Bankura						
	1952	1957	1962	1967	1969	1971	1972	1952	1957	1962	1967	1969	1971	1972
Congress (1)	**35.4**		35.1	**46.4**	32.0	13.0	**56.3**	26.5	**23.5**	33.6	**30.9**	27.7	**36.8**	**61.0**
Congress (2)									**19.4**					
Congress (O)						6.7							2.2	
Bangla Congress						25.5							6.6	
CPI (1)	28.4		**52.7**					27.7	12.8	**34.4**	30.8	**58.3**	23.5	
CPI (2)									11.9					
CPM				43.0	**60.6**	**46.4**	43.7						25.2	35.4
SSP											3.4			
INDF					2.8									
Proutist					2.6									
Lok Dal					3.0							0.7		
Jana Sangh				10.6								6.6	2.6	
HMS (1)								**43.9**	15.4	32.0		6.3		2.3
HMS (2)									15.0					
Independents	21.5					8.4		1.8	2.1		20.9	0.5	3.2	1.3
	10.8										14.0			
	3.8													

Barjora 1957: (See Bankura)

BANKURA DISTRICT	239. ONDA							240. VISHNUPUR						
	1952	1957	1962	1967	1969	1971	1972	1952	1957	1962	1967	1969	1971	1972
Congress (1)	**19.2**	**52.5**	**45.2**	33.7	26.6	**52.7**		**23.2**	**27.0**	44.6	**49.4**	33.8	**31.7**	**58.5**
Congress (2)	**23.0**							**20.1**	**26.0**					
Congress (O)					5.1							9.0		
Bangla Congress			6.2	8.1							**53.7**	5.3		
CPI	12.4							14.2	12.0	**45.4**	12.6	21.7		
CPM						**38.8**	38.4				10.8		28.3	35.3
PSP			2.6	4.6				4.6	11.0					
Forward Bloc			**35.6**	7.0										
Socialist							1.0							
INDF				0.5								6.2		
Lok Dal				1.0										
Jana Sangh					1.3						2.4	3.5	4.0	4.1
HMS (1)	12.9	28.1		24.7	10.3	2.9		11.8	12.0	10.0		2.8		
HMS (2)	12.6							10.7	10.0					
Independents	7.9	14.2	41.1				5.0	8.9	2.0		15.1			2.1
	6.1	4.8	5.0		2.9			6.6			9.6			
	6.1	0.4												

BANKURA DISTRICT	241. KOTULPUR							242. INDAS						
	1952	1957	1962	1967	1969	1971	1972	1952	1957	1962	1967	1969	1971	1972
Congress	**79.2**	**79.8**	44.6	47.6	36.3	**68.7**		(See		31.3	37.6	37.1	**57.6**	
Congress (O)					3.6			Vishnupur						3.3
Bangla Congress			**46.6**	**51.3**	9.6			and		**68.7**	56.5	9.2		
CPI					12.2			Saltora)				11.2		
CPM			6.8		**38.4**	27.6							**42.4**	39.1
INDF				1.0								1.8		
Jana Sangh												0.8		
HMS	14.6	5.0												
Independents	6.2	15.2	2.0			3.7						3.3		

BANKURA DISTRICT	243. SONAMUKHI							Others: SALTORA						
	1952	1957	1962	1967	1969	1971	1972	1952	1957	1962	1967	1969	1971	1972
Congress (1)	**20.3**	(See		**47.7**	38.3	36.0	**59.6**	**61.9**	(See Indas)					
Congress (2)	**20.3**	Patrasayer)												
Bangla Congress			23.7			8.1	2.9							
CPI					17.0					34.0				
CPM				28.6	**58.1**	**38.8**	37.4							
PSP (1)	8.7													
PSP (2)	6.9													
Forward Bloc (1)	6.8													
Forward Bloc (2)	6.2													
INDF					3.6									
Jana Sangh	7.6													
Independents	9.5									4.0				
	4.9									0.1				
	4.5													
	2.6													
	1.6													

BANKURA DISTRICT	Others: KHATRA							Others; PATRASAYER						
	1952	1957	1962	1967	1969	1971	1972	1952	1957	1962	1967	1969	1971	1972
Congress (1)	**19.7**							**26.0**	**56.8**					
Congress (2)	14.4	(See Kotulpur)						26.0	(See Sonamukhi)					
CPI (1)	10.7							24.0	43.2					
CPI (2)	9.9							17.0						
PSP (1)	6.8													
PSP (2)	6.6													
HMS (1)	**18.6**													
HMS (2)	13.3													
Independents								7.0						

BURDWAN DISTRICT	244. HIRAPUR							245. KULTI						
	1952	1957	1962	1967	1969	1971	1972	1952	1957	1962	1967	1969	1971	1972
Congress (1)	35.3	**49.8**	**38.3**	42.2	24.1	**48.6**		**22.1**	28.6	**39.3**	35.1	36.5	**38.8**	**59.5**
Congress (2)								**15.7**						
Congress (O)					2.8								4.1	
Bangla Congress					0.9						32.2		12.9	
CPI		35.7	17.4		27.0					30.0				
CPM			36.5	**57.8**	**45.2**	46.1							31.8	30.4
PSP (1)		11.8	2.9					8.4	**48.9**	25.4				
PSP (2)								2.3						
SSP											32.7	**60.7**	11.1	
Socialist						5.3								10.1
Jana Sangh	2.3		4.9						5.4					
INDF												2.8		
Independents	**55.6**	2.7						9.3	7.6	4.0			1.1	
	4.2							9.0	7.2	1.3				
	0.9							6.3	2.3					
	0.9							4.5						
	0.8							4.5						
								4.4						
								3.8						
								2.8						
								2.7						
								2.3						
								1.9						

BURDWAN DISTRICT	246. BARABANI							247. ASANSOL						
	1952	1957	1962	1967	1969	1971	1972	1952	1957	1962	1967	1969	1971	1972
Congress	37.4	**49.2**	38.8	33.4			**70.9**	25.5	**45.4**	27.7	**45.0**	41.0		
Congress (O)					2.0								12.3	
CPI	**43.1**	11.7		13.5				0.9	39.5	**43.7**	9.1		42.9	**58.7**
CPM		39.0	**61.3**	**48.6**	27.0						33.9	**55.9**	**44.7**	39.0
PSP	19.5									5.0				
Socialist						2.1								1.2
Forward Bloc								**40.1**						
Jana Sangh										2.4	2.2	3.1		1.2
SBP										8.0				
Independents						1.3	1.2	11.9	7.6	13.0	9.8			
								11.0	5.1	2.6				
								7.2						
								3.5						

BURDWAN DISTRICT	248. RANIGANJ							249. JAMURIA						
	1952	1957	1962	1967	1969	1971	1972	1952	1957	1962	1967	1969	1971	1972
Congress (1)	**16.3**		42.0	45.4	41.7	16.6	37.8	21.4	**57.0**	43.2	**50.7**	37.9	**58.3**	
Congress (2)	15.7							17.1						
Congress (O)						1.4							1.7	
Bangla Congress											3.0			
CPI		**52.8**			14.5									
CPM				**48.2**	**54.3**	**68.9**	**60.8**						**55.8**	41.7
Forward Bloc										10.0				
PSP (1)	5.2		5.2					**21.4**	33.0					
PSP (2)								16.6						
SSP											**53.9**	47.4	4.6	
Jana Sangh				6.5	4.0			3.3						
Independents	**27.4**							8.1			1.8			
	11.5							4.0						
	6.5							3.6						
	4.3							2.4						
	3.7							2.1						
	3.2													
	2.5													
	3.7													

(Raniganj PSP column notes: "(See Jamuria)")

BURDWAN DISTRICT	250. UKHRA							251. DURGAPUR						
	1952	1957	1962	1967	1969	1971	1972	1952	1957	1962	1967	1969	1971	1972
Congress				**46.9**	46.5	45.8	**61.3**		**57.1**	46.6	48.4			**55.9**
Congress (O)	(See											43.4		
Bangla Congress	Raniganj)			12.8										
CPI										3.8	7.4			
CPM				40.3	**53.5**	**54.2**	38.7			**49.6**	**51.6**	**49.1**	44.1	
PSP									18.3					
Worker's Party									3.5					
Forward Bloc									21.1					

BURDWAN DISTRICT	252. FARIDPUR							253. AUSGRAM						
	1952	1957	1962	1967	1969	1971	1972	1952	1957	1962	1967	1969	1971	1972
Congress (1)			46.9	46.8	21.8	**51.2**	**26.0**	**45.2**	29.0	38.8	35.6			49.7
Congress (2)							**24.0**							
Congress (O)					13.1	0.8							1.3	
Bangla Congress		**49.5**	**51.7**		3.3								35.2	
CPI					16.2								7.3	
CPM					41.2	45.4					51.9	60.1	56.1	50.3
PSP (1)								5.9						
PSP (2)								4.9						
RCPI				1.5										
Forward Bloc (1)								9.7	21.0	14.0				
Forward Bloc (2)								0.7						
PML												4.3		
Jana Sangh								3.9						
Independents		3.6			3.3	2.7		7.7	28.0	**31.1**	9.3			
					0.6			4.9	5.9	22.0				
								4.8		4.0				
								3.6						
								2.4						
								0.9						
								0.7						

BURDWAN DISTRICT	254. BHATAR							255. GALSI						
	1952	1957	1962	1967	1969	1971	1972	1952	1957	1962	1967	1969	1971	1972
Congress (1)	**49.4**	40.0	**38.2**	28.2			**72.7**	**22.9**	19.8	**54.8**	34.8	33.9		
Congress (2)							24.1	20.5						
Congress (O)					1.4								3.8	3.3
Bangla Congress					31.6								32.7	
CPI		**55.3**	36.1	**68.7**	13.6			19.1						**53.5**
CPM					46.8	27.3							56.6	43.2
PSP	34.0													
Forward Bloc								7.1	**20.5**	45.2			6.9	
RSP					6.6									
Lok Dal				2.3										
Jana Sangh (1)								4.1						
Jana Sangh (2)								3.6						
SBP			4.7											
Independents	11.1			25.7	0.8			19.2	**28.4**		**57.6**	**66.1**		
	5.4								6.1		7.6			
									4.7					

BURDWAN DISTRICT	256. BURDWAN NORTH							257. BURDWAN SOUTH						
	1952	1957	1962	1967	1969	1971	1972	1952	1957	1962	1967	1969	1971	1972
Congress			41.9	33.7		34.0	**67.7**			**45.7**	44.5		47.8	**71.7**
Congress (O)	(See					0.8		(See					1.5	
CPM	Burdwan)		**48.5**	**60.9**		**62.7**	32.3	Burdwan)		41.8	**55.5**		**50.1**	28.3
Forward Bloc			9.6			2.5								
Proutist				2.3										
Independents				3.1						12.5			0.6	

BURDWAN DISTRICT	258. KHANDAGHOSH							259. RAINA						
	1952	1957	1962	1967	1969	1971	1972	1952	1957	1962	1967	1969	1971	1972
Congress (1)	**37.0**		**53.0**	**45.0**	30.8	39.4	**62.8**	20.4	23.2	**65.8**	36.0	37.4	36.6	**56.4**
Congress (2)								20.1	22.6					
Congress (O)						1.7							3.2	
Bangla Congress						1.5								
CPM						51.2	37.2				23.4	**52.2**	**60.3**	43.6
PSP (1)			10.0					**21.2**	**27.8**	30.1	**37.9**	1.7		
PSP (2)								20.4	26.5					
SSP				40.4	**66.9**	0.7								
Forward Bloc				14.6										
Worker's Party			4.0											
INDF					2.3							8.7		
RSP						5.4								
Jana Sangh	5.9							1.7						
Bolshevik Party								0.9						
SBP			7.6											
Independents	31.4		19.0					4.6		4.2	2.7			
	17.8		5.0					4.1						
	4.2		1.4					3.5						
	3.7							1.8						
								1.4						

BURDWAN DISTRICT

	260. JAMALPUR							261. MEMARI						
	1952	1957	1962	1967	1969	1971	1972	1952	1957	1962	1967	1969	1971	1972
Congress			**77.6**	**64.5**	39.6	42.1	**65.9**	49.8	**49.8**	40.9		33.6		**80.2**
Congress (O)	(See					1.8		(See					0.8	
Bangla Congress	Kalna)				60.4	5.7		Kalna)						
CPI										50.2				
CPM				24.9							47.6	**58.7**	**62.4**	17.0
Forward Bloc											1.4			
Forward Bloc (M)			**50.4**											
PSP			22.4	10.6							1.4			
INDF												0.5		
Jharkhand													3.3	2.8
Independents							34.1							

BURDWAN DISTRICT

	262. KALNA							263. NADANGHAT						
	1952	1957	1962	1967	1969	1971	1972	1952	1957	1962	1967	1969	1971	1972
Congress (1)	**22.5**	21.2	43.0	44.9	43.0	42.6	**97.8**			**51.3**	45.9			**94.8**
Congress (2)	**19.6**	17.4						(See						
Congress (O)								Purbasthali)				38.8		
CPI (1)	19.2	**26.0**	**54.2**								7.1			
CPI (2)		**25.2**												
CPM				**47.6**	**57.0**	**54.4**	1.5			41.6	**53.5**	**59.6**		4.1
PSP	18.6			7.0										
INDF												0.6		
Jana Sangh	11.8													
Jharkhand					3.0									
Independents	2.5	7.5	2.8	0.6			0.7						1.6	1.1
	1.9	1.6												
	1.5	1.2												
	1.4													
	1.0													

BURDWAN DISTRICT	264. MANTESWAR							265. PURBASTHALI						
	1952	1957	1962	1967	1969	1971	1972	1952	1957	1962	1967	1969	1971	1972
Congress	**52.5**	43.9	48.4	**56.8**	37.2	33.9	**91.1**	**56.9**	**56.4**	**51.2**	43.1	45.7	32.4	**68.8**
Congress (O)						1.6	0.2						2.7	
Bangla Congress					3.8									
CPI			**51.6**							43.7	45.0			
CPM				37.4	**60.1**	**57.1**	8.7			**46.8**	**52.8**	**63.8**	31.2	
PSP	47.5										2.8	1.5	1.2	
Forward Bloc		11.1		5.8		3.6		8.3						
Lok Dal				2.2										
Jana Sangh								27.0				1.3		
Independents		**45.1**			0.6			7.7		3.8	5.9			

BURDWAN DISTRICT	266. KATWA							267. MANGALKOT						
	1952	1957	1962	1967	1969	1971	1972	1952	1957	1962	1967	1969	1971	1972
Congress	27.9	**54.5**	43.3	47.4	**51.4**	41.5	**60.4**	39.9		46.4	**52.4**	36.9		**57.1**
Congress (O)					3.8								1.8	2.2
Bangla Congress												36.2		
CPI	**35.1**	42.5	**56.7**							53.6				
CPM				**48.8**	47.3	**54.7**	39.6				47.6	**63.1**	**62.0**	40.8
Lok Dal					1.4									
Jana Sangh	9.7													
HMS	11.1	3.0												
Independents	10.2		2.2					32.6						
	3.3		1.6					14.0						
	2.7							8.3						
								3.9						
								1.3						

(267. MANGALKOT: See Ondal)

BURDWAN DISTRICT	268. KETUGRAM							Others : BURDWAN						
	1952	1957	1962	1967	1969	1971	1972	1952	1957	1962	1967	1969	1971	1972
Congress (1)	37.2	**27.5**	23.4	**52.6**	43.3	41.2	**63.2**	42.2	47.4	**67.7**				
Congress (2)		**30.5**									(See			
Congress (O)					1.7						Burdwan			
CPI (1)		13.0	**38.3**		13.7			**50.9**	**48.6**	31.0	North			
CPI (2)		11.5									and			
CPM				47.5	**56.7**	**43.4**	36.8				South)			
PSP	6.0													
Forward Bloc	8.3													
Worker's Party										0.7				
Jana Sangh									3.9					
HMS (1)	**37.4**	9.5						5.5						
HMS (2)		5.5												
SBP										0.6				
Independents	11.1	2.5	26.2					1.4						
		12.1												

BURDWAN DISTRICT	Others : ONDAL						
	1952	1957	1962	1967	1969	1971	1972
Congress (1)	**27.7**						
Congress (2)	**28.6**						
CPI (1)	19.7						
CPI (2)	15.7						
Independents	5.2						
	1.8						
	1.3						

BIRBHUM DISTRICT	269. NANUR							270. BOLPUR						
	1952	1957	1962	1967	1969	1971	1972	1952	1957	1962	1967	1969	1971	1972
Congress (1)	**18.5**			**43.9**	37.3		**58.5**	**18.0**	**54.8**	33.6	45.2	37.0		
Congress (2)	**16.8**	(See						17.2						
Congress (O)		Suri)			2.2									9.9
Bangla Congress			19.5		33.7							33.4		
CPI (1)	15.1				14.0			5.8				21.3	**48.7**	
CPI (2)	14.7							4.4						
CPM			36.6	**57.7**	**50.2**	41.5							**39.8**	38.2
PSP (1)	3.5							7.0			1.0	3.8		
PSP (2)								5.7						
PSP (3)								5.3						
PSP (4)								3.2						
Socialist														1.1
RSP								1.4	23.4	**66.5**	**53.0**	60.6		
RCPI	4.0													
INDF					1.8							1.0		
Proutist					2.0									
HMS (1)	15.3							11.3	21.8					
HMS (2)								7.8						
PML													0.5	
Independents	8.1				1.2			5.4			1.8		1.6	2.0
	2.1							4.9						
	1.9							2.3						

BIRBHUM DISTRICT	271. LABHPUR							272. DUBRAJPUR						
	1952	1957	1962	1967	1969	1971	1972	1952	1957	1962	1967	1969	1971	1972
Congress		45.3	29.0	**59.2**	41.4	17.1			42.8	28.3	34.2	20.8	**53.9**	
Congress (O)						3.4							3.3	
Bangla Congress						22.6								
CPI	(See Nanur)	**47.1**	37.8			50.5								
CPM				40.8	**52.6**	**50.3**	49.5						**40.7**	
Forward Bloc									**57.2**	35.5	**45.7**	17.8	46.1	
RSP												15.0		
INDF					3.3									
HMS		7.6												
PML					2.7									
Independents			33.2		6.6				**36.3**	16.4	2.4			
												3.7		

BIRBHUM DISTRICT	273. RAJNAGAR							274. SURI						
	1952	1957	1962	1967	1969	1971	1972	1952	1957	1962	1967	1969	1971	1972
Congress (1)		**24.6**	36.4	45.3	41.5	37.2	**52.7**	**19.2**	10.1	**51.5**	**37.3**	41.3	18.1	**56.0**
Congress (2)		**23.2**						**19.2**	13.5					
Congress (O)						4.4								
Bangla Congress													20.3	
CPI									**25.5**					
CPM						**38.9**							23.2	
PSP		20.8						17.0	**30.1**	19.0	26.3			
Forward Bloc	(See Khayrasole)	21.2	**47.2**	**46.0**	**47.5**	19.5	47.3	15.1						
RSP										3.5				
SUC										21.0	36.3	**57.4**	**34.5**	44.0
INDF					0.5									
HMS			9.8											
Swatantra										5.0				
PML												1.3		
Independents		10.2	3.6	5.1	10.5			12.5	10.7				**3.8**	
			3.0	3.6				4.9	4.8					
								3.9	3.6					
								3.8	1.7					
								2.4						
								1.8						

BIRBHUM DISTRICT	275. MAHAMMAD BAZAR							276. MAYURESWAR						
	1952	1957	1962	1967	1969	1971	1972	1952	1957	1962	1967	1969	1971	1972
Congress		**44.9**	**53.7**	42.5	28.4		**54.7**			41.2	**50.9**	30.6	34.6	
Congress (O)					3.7								2.2	2.4
Bangla Congress			39.9	**48.2**	14.9									
CPI		28.6								**44.5**	19.3		**35.1**	**50.7**
CPM					**45.6**		45.3				24.6	**56.1**	28.0	46.9
PSP		15.0		1.6										
Proutist												0.8		
PML				7.8								12.5		
Independents		8.1	6.4		6.4					10.0	5.2			
		1.9			1.0					2.3				
		1.5								2.0				

BIRBHUM DISTRICT	277. RAMPURHAT							278. HANSAN						
	1952	1957	1962	1967	1969	1971	1972	1952	1957	1962	1967	1969	1971	1972
Congress (1)	24.1	15.3	**49.8**	25.7	38.2	36.0	**53.8**			**41.8**	25.6	23.6		57.2
Congress (2)	21.7	13.7												
Congress (O)					3.9								2.6	0.8
CPI		**18.7**												
CPM				16.5		**50.4**	43.4							
Forward Bloc (1)	**24.9**		35.7	**35.6**	**57.4**	9.8					25.5	**47.2**	8.3	
Forward Bloc (2)	**23.7**													
RCPI													44.2	42.0
INDF				0.5								0.2		
Proutist				1.2										
Jana Sangh		1.7		2.7								8.4		
HMS (1)		5.0												
HMS (2)		4.8												
PML												18.6		
Independents	5.5	**31.2**	11.6	22.2		2.9					32.1		21.3	
		6.5	1.9								0.7			
		1.3	1.0											
		1.3												
		0.7												

BIRBHUM DISTRICT	279. NALHATI							280. MURARAI						
	1952	1957	1962	1967	1969	1971	1972	1952	1957	1962	1967	1969	1971	1972
Congress (1)	**34.7**	**22.6**	**42.8**	23.0	32.9	14.5	35.3	24.1		35.3	39.2	43.6	15.7	**65.6**
Congress (2)		**17.8**												
Congress (O)					5.1	5.9								1.4
Bangla Congress											0.7	15.0		
PSP		1.3	28.0				**25.8**	26.3						
Forward Bloc		7.6		9.3			1.9							
RSP									**38.4**					
SUC							17.9				**41.4**	**54.1**	**53.7**	29.5
INDF												1.0		
Proutist				1.8								0.2		
Lok Dal				4.4										
HMS	21.7	4.8	0.6											
PML												1.0		
Muslim League						9.9								
SBP		3.6												
Independents	19.2	13.0	25.0	**27.4**	**53.7**	**39.7**	**46.1**	15.0			18.7		14.2	4.9
	13.7	9.3		20.1	7.2	22.8	2.7	13.0						
	7.8	6.4		14.4				11.5						
	1.7	6.2		5.7				5.3						
	1.3	4.5						3.0						
		3.2												
		2.5												
		0.8												

See Nalhati

BIRBHUM DISTRICT	*Others :* KHAYRASOLE						
	1952	1957	1962	1967	1969	1971	1972
Congress	**28.2**						
PSP (1)	27.2	(See Rajnagar)					
PSP (2)	10.5						
HMS	26.2						
Independents	7.9						